PRAISE FOR

"Amos Smith's unique voice is rooted in his long-term centering prayer practice and his international background. *Be Still and Listen* is a trumpet call to the inner treasures of contemporary Christian mysticism."
                    —RICHARD ROHR,
                        author of *Falling Upward*

"In a lively, accessible, and masterful style Amos Smith unveils the mystical foundations of Christianity and the spiritual wealth found in Scripture."
                    —KYRIACOS MARKIDES,
                        author of *The Mountain of Silence*

"*Be Still and Listen* promises to be a refreshing companion to your spiritual journey, helping you to deepen your capacity for presence of being, assisting you to live in the here and now, and guiding you along the mystical path with Christ."
                    —PHILEENA HEUERTZ,
                        author of *Pilgrimage of a Soul*

"Amos Smith's mystical writing builds bridges between Eastern and Western Christianity."
                    —ABBA YOHANNES,
                        Ethiopian Orthodox monk

"*Be Still and Listen* has made me think deeply about my own spiritual life and practice. I am confident that this important book will have a similar impact on you."

—DALE HANSON BOURKE,
author of *Embracing Your Second Calling*

"Amos Smith reminds us that the path of centering prayer and Christian mysticism is not a race. It's a marathon. As many Scriptures attest, our relationship with God requires patient waiting in stillness and silence, day after day, month after month, year after year. The marvel is that in time God will transform us!"

—RICH LEWIS,
author and centering prayer workshop leader

"Our hearts hunger, our souls thirst, for the freedom and spiritual life that existed in the Garden—of walking close to God in the cool of the evening and being whole. Amos Smith shows us how we can recover a portion of that in our interior lives now."

—J. BRENT BILL,
Quaker author of *Holy Silence*

BE STILL AND LISTEN

Experience the Presence of God in Your Life

Amos Smith

Foreword by Phileena Heuertz
Afterword by Dale Hanson Bourke

PARACLETE PRESS
BREWSTER, MASSACHUSETTS

2018 First Printing

Be Still and Listen: Experience the Presence of God in Your Life

Copyright © 2018 by Amos Smith

ISBN 978-1-61261-865-4

Library of Congress Cataloging-in-Publication Data:
    Names: Smith, Amos (Pastor), author.
    Title: Be still and listen : experience the presence of God in your life /
        Amos Smith ; foreword by Phileena Heuertz ; afterword by Dale Hanson
        Bourke.
    Description: Brewster, MA : Paraclete Press, Inc., 2018. | Includes
        bibliographical references.
    Identifiers: LCCN 2018006158 | ISBN 9781612618654 (trade paper)
    Subjects: LCSH: Mysticism. | Contemplation. | Listening--Religious
        aspects--Christianity. | Spiritual life--Christianity.
    Classification: LCC BV5082.3 .S63 2018 | DDC 248.2/2--dc23
    LC record available at https://lccn.loc.gov/2018006158

10 9 8 7 6 5 4 3 2 1

Published by Paraclete Press
Brewster, Massachusetts
www.paracletepress.com

Printed in the United States of America

Dedicated to my parents, Susan Miner Smith
and Edward Hamilton Smith Jr.,
whose infinite patience and fierce love sustained me.

CONTENTS

FOREWORD

When a client meets with me for spiritual direction, we usually begin with a prayer I learned from a beloved teacher who Amos and I share, Richard Rohr. The prayer is based on Psalm 46:10. By repeating the following five consecutively diminishing sentences, the client and I are assisted in coming into Presence of Being.

> Be still and know that I am God
> Be still and know that I am
> Be still and know
> Be still
> Be

Presence of mind, heart, and body is not so easy for us to experience. We live most of life ruminating or reminiscing over past events, and dreading or planning future ones. And yet, God cannot be experienced in the past or in the future, only in the present moment. Sure, we can remember past experiences of God or anticipate future ones, but we can only be in God, right here, right now. This is what the mystics have proclaimed for centuries; that Christian faith is about living in and with our Creator. The more we can live in the present moment, the more we can encounter God and the transformation that such an encounter catalyzes.

As Amos points out in the subsequent pages, establishing presence of mind, heart, and body in God is like being anchored in our center of gravity. Our center of gravity is the awareness that in God we live and move and have our being (Acts 17:28), and nothing can separate us from the love of God (Rom. 8:39). So, regardless of circumstances and surrounding chaos, we are established in the absolute, unchanging God, who has got us.

From our center, we can then respond to life in cooperation with the Divine from our true or higher self, rather than from our false or small self who has a habit of making things worse instead of better. This is what transformation looks like.

So how do we access such freedom? How do we move beyond categorical belief systems of the mind, to companioning and cooperating with the Source of our being? Amos aptly tells us, "It's only in pure faith, a groping in the dark, and an acceptance of utter unknowing and mystery, that we taste some portion of that vast primordial freedom!"[1] The way of the mystic is the way of unknowing, darkness, and pure faith because the mystic relinquishes control.

The English word "mystic" is derived from the Greek words *muein*, meaning close the eyes or lips, and *mustes*, meaning an initiated person. Essentially, the mystic is one who lets go of control ("close eyes and lips") and lets God bring her into the secrets and mysteries of God's reign (initiated person). Jesus said this is the way into the Kingdom of God. The way is about letting go, trusting, and being led, like a child (Matt. 18:3), like a grain of wheat (John 12:24), like an old man (John 21:18).

This kind of radical faith requires trust.

Amos writes, "People trust God as long as they're in control. Then, as soon as they lose control, they lose faith. This kind of faith bullies God to conform to our plans. God becomes the ultimate spotter." This kind of faith doesn't require trust. And this kind of faith won't lead a person into primordial freedom. That's why throughout these pages, Amos earnestly exhorts us to let go of control! Trust God! And then you'll be free!

Amos knows what he's talking about. Years of devoted centering prayer practice has helped Amos realize that freedom in Christ is not a belief or behavior system, but a radical shift of consciousness. Most of us live from a place of spiritual un-consciousness. Freedom is accessed as we become conscious.

And as Amos points out, there are many ways to wake up or become conscious. A spiritual practice such as centering prayer is incredibly helpful, as is fishing or knitting for some people. Whatever practice helps our ego relinquish its dominance and move away from the center makes room for transformation and freedom to emerge in our lives. One of my and Amos's other beloved teachers, Thomas Keating, puts it this way: "The Transforming Union is the restructuring of consciousness, not just an experience, or set of experiences."[2]

If you have already stepped onto the mystical path in Christ, these pages will support your evolving consciousness, helping you to be more rooted in your center of gravity. And if you think Christian mysticism is only for a select few, Amos's reflections will reveal how utterly human the mystical journey with Christ really is and how we all have access to it.

But don't think for a moment that mysticism is high, lofty, and disengaged from the real world. Amos is sure to remind us that as we deepen conscious union with God, the Divine life flows more freely through us for the healing of our world. In essence, unitive consciousness helps us integrate contemplation and action in a form of contemplative activism for the common good.

Be Still and Listen promises to be a refreshing companion to your spiritual journey, helping you to deepen your capacity for presence of being, assisting you to live in the here and now, and guiding you along the mystical path with Christ.

—Phileena Heuertz
Author of *Pilgrimage of a Soul: Contemplative Spirituality for the Active Life*
Co-founder, Gravity, a Center for Contemplative Activism

PREFACE

Be still, and know that I am God.
—Psalm 46:10 (RSV)

Extreme importance [is] attached by the Desert tradition
to . . . the quality of stillness and silence.
—Kallistos Ware[3]

David, who according to biblical tradition wrote the Psalms, was a shepherd. Moses, who inspired the first five books of the Bible, spent much of his life as a shepherd. Samuel, Samson, and John the Baptist were ascetics.

The great prophets of the Hebrew Scriptures, Elijah and Elisha, were reclusive and mysterious. Other prophets of the Hebrew Scriptures, such as Isaiah and Hosea, likewise seem to have had monastic, or at least deeply ascetic, leanings. The Greek Testament tells us that Jesus "often withdrew to lonely places and prayed," sometimes prayed all night, and "fasted in the wilderness for forty days and forty nights" (see Lk. 5:16, 6:12). Most of the scribes who copied the Scriptures by hand for centuries were monastic.[4]

In other words, they were all people accustomed to spending successive days and hours of solitude steeped in silence. This was their context. This is what I call the inherent mysticism of the Bible. Many of the people who wrote and inspired the Bible were steeped in silence and stillness. This is the premise of *Be Still and Listen*.

The essence of the deepest prayer forms of Christianity are silence and stillness. Many have inherited this essence today in the practice of centering prayer. Silence and stillness are the primary language of mystics past and present. Luminaries have drawn from the silence, stillness, and mysticism in Scripture for millennia. To see for yourself, turn to these Scriptures, for instance, that celebrate silence: Proverbs 10:19, Proverbs 17:28, Job 13:15, Matthew 27:11, Mark 14:61, and Luke 23:9. Then, turn to these that celebrate stillness: 1 Kings 19:12 (KJV), Psalm 23:2, Psalm 46:10, and Mark 4:39.

Most of all, to receive the Spirit that inspired Scripture we each need to learn to cultivate silence and stillness in our lives. We need to learn to be still. It was in stillness that deep listening led to illumined Scripture, and it is in deep listening today that our lives can be illuminated.

How to Use This Book

You can treat this book as a daily devotional. Each section is a self-contained unit and only takes a few minutes to read, so you could easily read a section a day or a chapter a week.

Another approach is to use the selected Bible verses as focal points for *Lectio Divina*.[5] Then, depending on the style of your group, the meditations could serve as catalysts for conversation.

To assist dialogue and small group study I conclude each chapter with questions for reflection and discussion.

For translations of Bible verses I've depended primarily on The Message and the New International Version, with other translations sprinkled in. Whenever easily accomplished, I have made Scripture passages gender inclusive. I have referenced Bible translations as follows:

AIV	An Inclusive Version	Oxford University Press
KJV	King James Version
MSG	The Message
NIV	New International Version
NKJV	New King James Version
NLT	New Living Translation
NRSV	New Revised Standard Version
RSV	Revised Standard Version
WEB	World English Bible

Where not otherwise marked, Scripture translations are my own.

When telling stories, I use fictitious names to protect identities. I encourage the reader to flow with the text. Then, at the end, if you have interest, you can peruse them. Some endnotes are significant for grasping the subjects at hand, especially those that appear beside headings or subheadings. All books listed in the notes are also listed with more detail in the bibliography.

Disclaimers

1. Accusations of derangement seem to be an occupational hazard of Christian mystics dating back to at least the sixth century. Maximus the Confessor writes, "For he who has been united with the truth has the assurance that all is well with him, even though most people rebuke him for being out of his mind. For without their being aware he has moved from delusion to the truth of real faith; and he knows for sure that he is not deranged, as they say. . . ."[6]

As Maximus writes, people have often thought mystics were out of their minds. People have often drawn targets on the backs of mystics and at times fired ammunition into those targets. Given this, it is important to clarify Christian mysticism's rightful place at the center of Christian tradition, beginning with Jesus. That is one of the aims of this book.

2. This is not an exegetical work. I have only sporadically consulted Bible commentaries. This book isn't about the fancy footwork of a reasoning mind that applies its rigor to Scripture. It is about intimacy with God and deep reflection.

3. Sometimes when we read a passage of the Bible intently and from the depths of our awareness, we can't help digging through our own souls to find a reference point. So in this book I often reflect on the Bible in the context of my life.

Why do I tell personal stories? I'm influenced by author Frederick Buechner, who often writes that teachers must tell personal stories of faith. Otherwise people will get the unfortunate message that faith is a two-thousand-year-old story preserved in the Bible, but not a living, contemporary reality.

4. When it comes to biblical interpretation I prefer the boyish optimism and exuberance of the mystic to the cautious plodding of the consummate academic. I have not exchanged the thrill of aliveness I see in my eight-year-old boy for dull domesticity (Lk. 18:16).

5. Some who have written about mysticism in Scripture have focused on the Gospel of John. There is precedent for this. Many commentators from both East and West agree that John is the most mystical of the Gospels. Yet, this approach is too narrow in scope for this book. In this book, my aim is to tease out the inherent mysticism throughout the Bible.[7]

6. There are some recurring themes in the chapters below, such as the general upheaval of our times. Repetition in the best sense is not cumbersome, but probes a challenging subject from a number of angles. With each repetition, different nuances and more clarity emerge.

INTRODUCTION

The spiritual journey, as I have experienced it, has not been about comfort. It's been about the birth of wonderment. My journey has been about letting go of everything I've known for an exquisite Unknown—for a delicious Mystery that keeps me baffled and babbling.

My approach has come from my conviction that the most mature among us are comfortable and at home in ambiguity and mystery. Demanding half-baked answers is a form of dysfunction and dis-ease.

The mystic John of the Cross stood out from the crowd. As a result, he spent years in a dank, dirty dungeon. Mysticism is threatening to the crowd. Henry David Thoreau was called a mystic. And in the next breath he was called a malcontent and a gadfly.

To blend in with the crowd is safe and at first it is preferred. Yet, the beauties of sustained practiced mysticism give us the courage to stand out—not because we want to make some social statement. We have the courage to stand out because we have slowly come to accept our uniqueness. Before our forays into mystic silences and retreats from the crowd we feared our uniqueness. We wanted to simply play along and fit in. Then, in time, we finally experienced the deep affirmation that allowed us to celebrate our distinct selves.

In mystic communion, we gain unshakable assurance that God celebrates our uniqueness. Then we come to celebrate it. We also come to celebrate the uniqueness of others. We come to a genuine appreciation of diversity. We give up the need for others to conform to this standard or that. We discover the inexhaustible, inclusive love of God, which includes us, of all people. From that standpoint, we want to share what we have been given, even if it makes us stand out, even if it invites hardship.

We journey toward knowing the truth and living in the freedom of that truth (John 8:32). This truth is subtle and hidden. It's the still small voice of a wanderer, not the big primetime voice of a newscaster (1 Kgs. 19:12).

Don't get me wrong. I have not arrived at the mysterious Light. But I am on a journey of perpetual arriving. Each time I peel another layer off the onion, only to discover that there is another, then another. Still, there are times when the Light is all-pervasive and I feel that I am indeed home. My writing then flows from a yearning to share that exquisite homeland. May we find that homeland together, not you in front and me behind, and not me in front and you behind, but side-by-side.

The Lobsters Analogy

In the nineteenth century lobsters were so plentiful in New England that they became a nuisance. They got caught in fishnets and washed up on beaches. They were so abundant that people shoveled them onto their fields for fertilizer.

Only the poor, who had no other options, ate lobster. Imagine that! A dramatic shift happened in the twentieth century. All of a sudden, people got a taste for lobsters and they became gourmet. New England fishermen figured out how to ship them, and they introduced them to the rest of the country, and the world, as "rare" and "precious." What happened with lobsters is true of Scripture.

The Bible can feel commonplace, old hat. Colleagues in ministry confide in me that Bible verses feel like nuisance lobsters shoveled out at church services.

Part of why the Bible can feel cumbersome and unsavory is because, especially in Protestant history, it has been used by dualistic minds to prove who is right. The ego's need to be right, to prove that it has the correct interpretation, created a monster that divided and re-divided the Church. In other words, the book of poetry that ultimately points to the love of Jesus and to justice for the oppressed became a wedge to divide us. This led to over thirty thousand Christian denominations worldwide.

The divisive legalistic approach to the Bible baffled mystics through the ages. It led mystics to pronounce, "Why has Christianity preferred the courtroom to the bridal chamber?"

The focal point of the Bible should be the marriage of the soul to God—the unity of Jesus's divinity and humanity, which can be mirrored in us. The passionate romance of the Song of Songs[8] should be central, not legal deliberations.

But, of course, the problem is not the Bible, just as the problem was not the lobsters. The problem is our approach to Scripture and the way it's taught. I resonate with author Kathleen Norris: "Children . . . begin to reject both poetry and religion for similar reasons, because the way both are taught takes the life out of them."[9]

The unitive, compassionate mind of Christ illumines the Bible for us, not the dualistic egotistic mind (Phil. 2:5). In other words, Scripture doesn't need to change any more than nineteenth-century lobsters needed to change. The way we see the Bible needs to change. This book is about reading Scripture with a mystical mind—a mind that's open to non-dual thinking and to Mystery.

It is not only the Scriptures themselves that are mystical. The state of our mind that we bring to Scripture can be mystical. Our perspective will determine whether or not we "see" (or interpret) that portion of the Scriptures as mystical or not.

If I have a hammer in my hand, I tend to approach everything as if it were a nail. In the same way, if my frame of reference is holistic, which is another name for mystical, when I read Scripture, I will see it as a whole. The words and sentences will have a synthetic quality because the nature of my mind is synthetic.

This book has to do with the Scriptures selected. It also has to do with a particular approach. When we are absorbed in desert solitude, silence, and stillness, we begin to see and understand the books, chapters, and verses of the Bible in a whole new way.

Part One:

ENTERING
THE
DESERT

Jesus often withdrew to lonely places and prayed.

—LUKE 5:16

*Jesus fasted in the wilderness for
forty days and forty nights.*

—MATTHEW 4:1–2

CHAPTER 1

Awareness, Deep Listening, and Contemplation and Action

Awareness

Now the earth was formless and empty, darkness was over the surface of the deep, and the Spirit of God was hovering over the waters. And God said, "Let there be light," and there was light. God saw that the light was good, and God separated the light from the darkness. God called the light "day," and the darkness God called "night." And there was evening, and there was morning—the first day.
—Genesis 1:2–5 (NIV)

Something subtle and profound makes us uniquely human. Something illusive yet extraordinarily powerful animates human genius. In its pure form, it "hovered over the surface of the deep" (Gen. 1:2). At the world's genesis, it separated the day and the night by name. It's a power that arrives at the age of reason (usually about twelve or thirteen). It is what some refer to as "full reflective self-consciousness." This is a more technical phrase for the familiar term, awareness.

I am amazed how many times people can hear the word awareness without fully recognizing its penetrating primal meaning. For a long time, I thought I knew how to grasp it. I thought I was aware. Only recently, however, I've discovered how little I can claim hold of this illusive powerhouse term.

I, like so many people, regularly slip into unconsciousness. On some level I tune out, space-out, check-out. "Out" is the key word. I'm no longer present. If there was a roll call, an astute observer would record "absent" after my name.

There are many intervals throughout the day when I check out. When I make my breakfast, I'm most often absent. I've made breakfast so many times in the same way that now I can do it in my sleep. When I sit down to eat after a long day I sometimes pull my chair without thinking—it's unconscious. I'm not aware of what I'm doing. Then I chew my food while thinking about something else, without tasting it.

When I sit in front of the television, like so many Americans, I check out. I just take in the sound bites and the newscaster's glossing of the news. I don't think about what comes into my senses. I allow mental laziness to creep over me. I just accept what's said wholesale, even when it insults my intelligence.

It's always easier to tune out. It is always easier not to question—to just accept what we are fed through mass media. It's always easier not to look beneath the surface, not to listen when it stretches or hurts, not to be present when we pull up a chair. It's also easier not to check in on our familiar destructive habits. It's easier just to let things slide. We effortlessly pop the tranquilizer that shuts off awareness. We switch to auto-pilot.

It's always easier to cut class, but when we get older we can no longer obtain the permission slip to be absent. We no longer have an excuse to simply check out. To be an adult in the best sense is to be present. It is to be attentive to our children, to the written and spoken word, to dinner, to brushing teeth, and to our world.

Even when we read, we are distracted and check out for a paragraph or two. This is normal. But, do we know that we have checked out and do we know which sentences we missed and why? Or are we so absent, we don't even know that we're absent?

When people check out and appeal to instinct, our world turns to indifference, apathy, bigotry, and violence. But when people check in and appeal to reason, our world turns to beauty, new mystical ways of understanding, compassionate responses to life, and simple poise.

"Let there be light," God said in Genesis chapter one. Roll call. Are you in or out?

▪ Deep Listening, Part 1

If you love me, keep my commandments. I will pray to God, who will give you another Counselor that he may be with you forever,—the Spirit of truth, whom the world can't receive; for it doesn't see him, neither knows him. You know him, for he lives with you, and will be in you. I will not leave you orphans. I will come to you.
—John 14:15–18 (WEB)

Ruth specializes in family counseling. One time I asked her, "What makes a good counselor?" She said, "Foremost, a good counselor listens deeply."

I asked Ruth what this deep listening looks like. She said that after a client finishes speaking, she takes a long pause, then rephrases what the client has said in a fresh way to give assurance that she had listened.

In Ruth's estimation, a good counselor only speaks about five percent of the time. "Mostly a good counselor just listens." What a gift. If only there were more good listeners in the world, there would be much greater understanding.

Listening skills make the Holy Spirit the Counselor in our lives (John 14:16). As a result of deep listening the Counselor understands our hearts.

Sometimes I think I've listened and I think I understand when I don't. Not so with the Counselor. The Counselor understands our false self, our pretensions, our evasions, our self-centered motivations. The Counselor is not fooled even when we manage to fool ourselves. The Counselor's deep subconscious knowing reveals itself in dreams, when we're on a morning run, or in conversation.

The Counselor listens deeply to our lives, and then at times, if we listen, the Counselor ever so gently nudges us. Sometimes the nudge is as simple as a phone call to make, an email to write, or a person to meet. Sometimes it's as easy as making a list of "things I am working on now." An item on my list as I write this is to listen deeply.

My intention when a parishioner named Paul walks into my office is to set aside everything else and give him my full, undistracted presence. My intent is to focus on his eyes, the contours of his forehead, his words, the tone and inflection of each word as it leaves his mouth, his body language. My intent is to reprogram. "This time is about you, you matter to me. I am listening to every word you say. I have abandoned my interior dialogue. I have dropkicked the distractions that vie for my attention, because in this moment you matter more to me than anything else." That's my intention, but I haven't realized such exquisite attentiveness.

On my best days, the person I listen to becomes the focus of my meditation.

Has someone ever focused on you with undivided attention? Such listening can create a space for words that have never been spoken before, for transformation. That's how the Counselor listens to us—inviting our true self to make an appearance. "Attention is the rarest and purest form of generosity," said the philosopher Simone Weil.

Deep Listening, Part 2

Ruth's counseling, which puts deep listening first, is instructive. How do we find the path to God and how do we stay on it? Listen deeply, and in the silence of our hearts the Counselor will speak.

This is demanding. How can we silence the din around us and in our minds long enough to listen deeply? And if we do make the time and have the patience to listen deeply, are we sure we'll hear the Spirit?

I visited my ninety-eight-year-old grandfather in New York City. It took patience to listen to him. And even then I missed a number of his words. It was only when I leaned in with my ear next to his lips that I understood more. He spoke in a whisper. To hear the counsel of the

Holy Spirit we have to lean in. Like my grandfather, the Counselor speaks in hushed tones.

Sometimes in prayer we feel as if we're leaning in to listen carefully, but to an empty chair. At that point, we feel we've entered into a one-way conversation. We sometimes feel we're "talking to the wall."

Teresa of Avila wrote, "The biggest mistake we make in prayer is praying as if God is absent." This is the problem we encounter. We're immersed in a culture of doubt. We have no reason to believe that there is a deeper truth beyond our senses. All we have ever known is our senses.

The turning point in prayer is when we finally stop talking, then stop thinking. Then we slowly begin to trust that the Counselor is there. Then, we lean in and listen for as long as it takes. As we wait, the empty chair begins to feel occupied. We feel the warm breath against our cheek. We brush up against an actual Being. We glimpse the Ancient One who was sitting there all along. We commune with the Counselor—the Ancient of Days (Dan. 7:9, 22).

Deep Listening, Part 3

No one can see shortwaves. They are imperceptible to the eye. Yet, if you have a shortwave radio, you can receive those shortwaves. Similarly, no one can see the Ancient Counselor. But if we dial in long enough and listen with our whole hearts we begin to perceive the Counselor's presence. Just as the wine taster's palate needs to be trained to decipher wine nuances, so too the spiritual faculties need to be trained to hear the Counselor's fine-tuned frequencies.

The Counselor requires wait time. When we exercise the patience to wait we gradually begin to hear a faint whisper like the still small voice that is mentioned in 1 Kings 19:12.

As we begin to hear the shortwaves come through the receiver, they may at first come through sporadically and with distortion. Patience is required.

When I was growing up overseas my dad tinkered with his short-wave radio, trying to get BBC news out of England. Sometimes he'd fiddle with the dials and antennas for a long time. Then the "aha" moment would come and a voice came through, crisp and clear.

If we persevere in prayer we will also reach that "aha" moment. And when the still small voice finally becomes audible we'll say, "I was deaf and now I hear. The ancient Counselor was there all along." "I hear BBC, even in this remote place."

Most people give up too soon. Don't! The essence of faith and trust is that an answer will come even when there's no sign of one.

Don't give up on the Holy Spirit. God's Counselor is our lifeline when everything else in life lets us down. Jesus says: "I will ask God and God will give you another Counselor, to be with you forever" (John 14:16). "I will not leave you desolate. I will come to you" (John 14:18). This is God's promise.

To listen deeply for the Counselor is a lifelong vocation. It is like seeking the best counselor, except you don't sit on a couch in a decorated office. You lie down in the grass. And instead of looking at a psychologist you look up at the stars.

The more we listen for the Counselor, the more comfortable we become in our own skin and the more at home we feel in our circumstances, whatever they may be. . . . Then we're less prone to distraction. And we feel less need to "get away." We're at home right here, right now.

It's normal to feel discontented and restless. That's the human condition. Yet, there is divine counsel. No matter what may go on in our lives and in the world, it's always available. It's not outside, but inside. And it's familiar. It belongs to us. It's our spiritual home.

■ Contemplation and Action, Part 1

Mary . . . sat before the Master (Jesus), hanging on every word he said. But Martha was pulled away by all she had to do in the kitchen. Later, she stepped in, interrupting them. "Master, don't you care that my sister has abandoned the kitchen to me? Tell her to lend me a hand."

The Master said, "Martha, dear Martha, you're fussing far too much and getting yourself worked up over nothing. One thing only is essential, and Mary has chosen it—it's the main course, and won't be taken from her."
—Luke 10:38–42 (MSG)

Mary and Martha symbolize the contemplative life and the active life.

We all have some sense of the active life. It's common. We know what it means to be busy. What we need to clarify is the contemplative life. It's a life of prayer, of reflection upon what matters. It's a life of wrestling with hard questions, a life that's familiar with silence and stillness and that accepts hardship.

Mary is the contemplative. She stills and empties herself in order to absorb Jesus's exquisite, transparent Presence, dipped in eternity, radiating primordial freedom. An artist carves out a bowl before we can put anything in it. A builder cuts out a window before we can see through it. We empty out the clutter in our minds before we are able to listen. A life of prayer makes room to listen. We empty ourselves like Mary.

Contemplation can be defined as progressively quieting the mind. Contemplatives can be counted on to listen because their minds aren't full. Their minds aren't preoccupied. They are not distracted by broken records that play in the background.

It's hard to describe someone who's at home with prayer. There's a quality about such people, a quiet composure and dignity. Someone who's at home in prayer knows three words: solidity, peace, and freedom. Prayer orders priorities. It connects us with the love of God so that we can reflect that love in a consistent and reliable way. To reflect that love does not require know-how. It requires letting go and getting out of the way so that Light can shine through.

Contemplatives are people like Mary, who prioritize their relationship with God, and who courageously back away from the relentless vacuum of deadening busyness. Mary put aside her "duties" and made Jesus the priority. Then Mary laid aside her thoughts and opened herself to Jesus's presence and utterances.

To lay aside thoughts is like training a puppy to sit in the center of a circle.[10] You gently bring the puppy to the center, then it wanders. Then you bring the puppy to the center again and it wanders again. This happens over and over. After a few days of this most people give up attempts to still the mind. Only after heaps of encouragement and determination will we stumble upon contemplation. Lo and behold, the puppy sits in the middle of the circle for an entire minute. This is a triumph! Then with time, the puppy sits for longer and longer periods. Slowly the mind finds deeper stability free of the constant wandering.

Augustine said, "Our hearts are restless until they find their rest in Thee, O God." So, prayer wades through the restlessness and distractions until we reach a still point. In that stillness we find what the book of Philippians refers to as "a peace that surpasses understanding" (Phil. 4:7). This is what Mary sought. For this we were created.

Thomas, a disciple of Jesus and the apostle to India, taught that there are three vocations. There's the active life, the contemplative life, and a mixture of the two. Thomas taught that the most exquisite path is the mixture. The contemplative life, focused primarily on liturgy and prayer, is suited to some, but is not the most balanced way. The active life, focused on work and efficiency, is also ultimately unbalanced. Thomas sought a combination of the two.

To skillfully serve God and each other we need a deep well of stillness and the unshakable interior resources that follow. From this interior well, we can drink and never grow thirsty (John 4:14). From this deep well of stillness we can satisfy the thirsts of this world. We can become people upon whom others can lean.

◼ Contemplation and Action, Part 2

I'm amazed how many times I've seen Mary and Martha referenced by the Desert Fathers and Mothers and by *The Philokalia* writers. Jesus's words, "Mary has chosen what is better," affirms a contemplative approach to living.

For the Desert Elders the Mary and Martha story affirms the decision to renounce all and enter the desert. In the twenty-first century, the story sometimes simply confirms the decision to renounce the laundry and sit on the cushion for twenty minutes.

It's not the desert, or the cave in the desert, or the cloister, or the monastery that ultimately matters. What matters is our desire to let go of all secondary busybody pursuits in order to pursue the spiritual life—in order to gaze upon Jesus, like Mary. "The hesychast, in the true sense of the word, is not someone who has journeyed outwardly into the desert, but someone who has embarked on the journey inwards into his [her] own heart," says Kallistos Ware.[11]

We strive for the integration of Mary and Martha. When steeped in the spirit of Mary, Martha's work is touched with the perfume of mindfulness. When contemplation infuses our actions, it adds artistry and elegance.

After many years of steering the Center for Action and Contemplation in Albuquerque, New Mexico, Richard Rohr now emphasizes the primary importance of contemplation. In the absence of the contemplative mind, activism can have the right objectives but the wrong spirit. In other words, activists can have the right goals. They might work for a worthy cause and commendable solutions. But they, themselves, don't embody the solution. Their presence makes people nervous. Their zeal isn't tempered with spaciousness, humor, and compassion.

In my own life, centering prayer and regular retreats are what keeps me balanced between Mary and Martha. When the two sisters are friends, I find that life becomes luminous and harmonious.

There's a reason why the Mary and Martha story appears directly after the story of the Good Samaritan (Lk. 10:25–37). The two narratives balance each other. The first is about solidarity with those who suffer. The second addresses the primacy of silent devotion to God.[12] Solitude and solidarity: a powerful duo.

A Quaker elder once told me, "There's one thing that's required of us: to do absolutely nothing and to do it very well." When we do absolutely nothing in solitude—when, after years of practice, all thoughts are but a distant planet—then another dimension of life opens. It is a holistic dimension in the bosom of God. Thoughts plunge us out of delicious union as the unknown fourteenth-century author of *The Cloud of Unknowing* writes: "God may be reached and held close by means of love, but by means of thought, never."[13]

Beyond thought, words, images, and sounds, there's unity. At first the unity feels like darkness. It's darkness to our reasoning minds—to the left brain, which distinguishes and verbalizes everything. But when we frequent that uncomfortable darkness, we find home.

In her book *Centering Prayer and Inner Awakening*, Cynthia Bourgeault writes that in the beginning the deep stillness of centering prayer is a place we go to. In time, it becomes a place we come from. It goes from foreign landscape to familiar homeland, like a lover who we've taken years to get to know.

Questions for Reflection and Discussion

1) How important is awareness to your everyday life? Please explain.

2) On a scale of 1 to 5 (5 being the highest) how would you describe your level of awareness?

3) When you compare the contemplative life and the active life do you think the contemplative life is "the better part"?

4) What does a contemplative life in the twenty-first century look like to you?

CHAPTER 2

◆ ——————— ◆

Centering Prayer

Set me free from the laziness that goes about disguised as activity when activity is not required. . . . Give me the strength that waits upon You in silence and peace.
—*Thomas Merton*[14]

Silence teaches us who we are.
—*Rich Lewis*[15]

Centering prayer, a term first coined by Thomas Merton, is a method of silent prayer with deep historic roots. Centering prayer is preserved in Western Contemplative tradition, most notably in *The Cloud of Unknowing* and in the teachings of John of the Cross and Teresa of Avila.

Centering prayer was made contemporary in recent decades by Basil Pennington, Thomas Keating, William Meninger, Cynthia Bourgeault, James Finley, David Frenette, Phileena Heuertz, Richard Rohr, and many others. Perhaps the fourth-century monk Evagrius gave the best description of all, calling centering prayer "the shedding of thoughts." It trains the mind to become free from thoughts and distractions so it can "rest in God" (Ps. 62:5).

A primary evangelical arm, so to speak, of contemporary centering prayer tradition is Contemplative Outreach, Ltd. Contemplative Outreach produces resources, facilitates centering prayer retreats worldwide, and administers a website.

Here is the best centering prayer advice I've received from seasoned practitioners over the years:

a) Do centering prayer at least twice a day for at least twenty minutes each time (the second time exponentially increases the long-term healing effects).

b) Do it at the same times every day, and on an empty stomach.

c) Daily silent prayer has a cumulative effect and requires steady practice for deep healing to take place—so give it time!

d) A regular exercise program speeds up centering prayer's long-term healing process.

e) Do at least one extended six- to ten-day centering prayer retreat yearly, if possible. This too, catapults progress.

Centering prayer has been the saving grace of my life. I say that because it has held me through everything. It held me through the death of my beloved mother and other major life transitions. Without it I would have been lost, with no refuge from the storm. The absolute simplicity and peace I found in centering prayer repeatedly drenched the thirsty pores of my body with profound contentment and homecoming. I repeatedly thought, *This experience is what I was created for. This divine union is all in all.* Centering prayer gave me an inexhaustible reservoir of hope (John 4:14).

"Prayer is not an individual but essentially a corporate activity: we pray always as members of one another in the Body of Christ. Even the hermit in the most remote corner of the desert, never stands before God alone, but always as one of a great family," writes Kallistos Ware.[16] The ultimate aim is not isolation but greater connection to the Christian community and to the human family.

Disciplined Silences, Part 1

And when you come before God, don't turn that into a theatrical production either. All these people making a regular show out of their prayers, hoping for stardom. Do you think God sits in a box seat?

Here's what I want you to do: Find a quiet, secluded place so you won't be tempted to role-play before God. Just be there as simply and honestly as you can manage. The focus will shift from you to God, and you will begin to sense his grace.

The world is full of so-called prayer warriors who are prayer-ignorant. They're full of formulas and programs and advice, peddling techniques for getting what you want from God. Don't fall for that nonsense. This is God you are dealing with, who knows better than you what you need.
—*Matthew 6:5–8* (MSG)

One beauty of long-term centering prayer practice is that it becomes easier and easier to stop obsessing and to consistently drop negative thought patterns. It also becomes easier to drop unnecessary activities from the calendar—to tell well-meaning solicitors "no" politely. It becomes easier to tell well-meaning people who need support for yet another project "no" politely and with kindness. In time, a regular centering prayer practice will bring greater trust in the entire process of letting go, even the end-game process of death and dying.[17]

Deuteronomy 6:4–5, which Jesus references in the Gospels, says, "Love the Lord your God with all your heart and with all your soul and with all your strength." How can we do this unless we first learn the ability to periodically clear our calendars and clear our thoughts? We can only give God our undivided attention after we set aside all other distractions.

Thomas Keating, a guiding light of the centering prayer movement, says that "Silence is God's first language, everything else is a poor translation." Another way to say this is, "Silence is God's first language, and everything else is a distraction."

Disciplined Silences, Part 2

But when you pray, go into your room, close the door and pray to God,
who is unseen. Then God, who sees what is done in secret, will reward you.
—Matthew 6:6 (NIV)

The scriptural basis of centering prayer passed down through generations of mystics is Matthew 6:6. Two saints of the Eastern Church, Dimitri of Rostov and Theophan the Recluse, both point to this verse as silent prayer's basis.[18] For Rostov the "room" in this verse means the heart. We shut the door to the heart and leave behind all the tangible senses.[19] We do this to open ourselves to what is ultimately real, and which lies beyond the senses.

The trouble is, we usually don't want to shut the door. We're enticed by the concert down the street, the new flavor of ice cream or frozen yogurt, the mind-blowing effects of that new movie we'd like to see, or see again. Our senses revel in the panoply of sights, smells, tastes, and sounds that we encounter. Paradoxically, however, the rapture that our souls are hardwired for is most available when we shut the doors to the senses. When we let go of the attractions to see this and taste that—then we become aware of another world.

This "other world" is like a deep-sea diver who visited the ocean's floor, got bored by it, and returned to the surface. "There is nothing happening down there," she told her friend. Then the friend said, "Go down to the ocean floor again. This time sit there for at least twenty minutes." The sea diver indulged her friend's request. Then an amazing thing happened. After she sat for about ten minutes the ocean floor sprang to life. Creatures she never saw before emerged from the rocks. Camouflaged sea creatures scurried beneath the sand. Those creatures hid because of all the commotion and fin flapping. When everything stilled, they finally felt safe enough to reveal themselves.

God is an introvert. Not only that, God is reclusive. I think of that wonderful description of God's whereabouts: "The secret place of the Most High" (Ps. 91:1). God doesn't reveal the depths of his/her self unless there is stillness and silence. And even then God's nature is retreating and illusive.

Elijah tried to get a glimpse of God and only heard "a still small voice" (1 Kgs. 19:12). Moses tried to get a glimpse and only saw God's back (Exod. 33:21–23). Don't ask me why. I'm a mild extrovert and have had to discipline myself to stay still long enough to hear a Word.

The unified and unifying dynamic Presence of the preexistent Word, which brought all the worlds into being, beckons. This Word holds the key to healing and integration, to ultimate relief from preoccupation with self and jags of divisive babble.

Waiting Patiently

I waited patiently for God;
God inclined to me and heard my cry.
God drew me up from the desolate pit,
out of the miry bog,
and set my feet upon a rock,
making my steps secure.
God put a new song in my mouth,
a song of praise to our God.
Many will see and be in awe,
and put their trust in God.
—*Psalm 40:1–3 (AIV)*

The lotus is a unique Asian flower often found in opaque, smelly bogs and swamps. The lotus stem starts at the floor of the bog or swamp, then grows through the muck and stench. When it finally surfaces on the top of the water it blossoms into a beautiful flower.

The flower's message: it's possible to rise through filth and stagnant water full of bacteria, decomposition, and disease. It's possible to rise through degenerate stink. Not only that, it's even possible to rise through all that, then blossom.

To use the analogy of Psalm 40, it's possible to get drawn up by the hand of God through the miry bog, then get set on a rock. It's possible to find a firm place to stand and blossom so that "many will see and fear."

The psalmist writes, "I waited patiently for the Lord." Volumes are packed into those six words. Wisdom is patience, delayed gratification, willingness to wait. The human mind can come up with a quick fix on the spot, but only fools are enticed by the whip of a tongue. Responses that bring healing, insight, and quality have waited for the counter-intuitive twist provided on an early-morning jog. Wisdom waits. We wait because the best response hasn't shown itself yet. We wait because we don't have a satisfactory response yet. We wait on the Lord.

"God raised me up out of the pit." Notice, it was not me, myself, and I. It was God who raised David out. In its own time the lotus rises. The timing is organic and can't be forced. The truth-teller is in the pit of our stomach, in our jaw muscle, or in between our shoulder blades. The truth-teller is muscle tension.

Throughout our lives when our needs weren't met, when we felt abandoned as children, when we weren't in control, when we suffered abuse, when our childhood insecurities overwhelmed us, when dad started to drink again, or when we got lost on the hike—whatever the traumas happened to be—they were all faithfully recorded in the muscles of our bodies in the form of tension. For most people these traumas are a garden variety. They are normal shocks to the nervous system that children experience growing up. Nonetheless, these shocks create tension, often profound tension, in the body.

The deep-seeded tensions in everyone's bodies are the actual "pit" of Psalm 40. These tensions lead to dysfunction, addiction, and over-compensating behavior to make up for perceived deprivations. If we wait patiently in silent prayer, in time the Lord will incline and hear our cries and lift us up and out, usually little by little over decades. When faithfulness to the life of prayer dissipates the tensions, we're raised up from the miry bog.

The daily discipline of centering prayer is the key that unlocks the tensions in our bodies.

Centering prayer is not easy. In fact, I wish it were easier. This is one of my struggles with God. Why does it take so long for the body to unwind the decades of built-up tension? Why does it take the lotus so long to slowly emerge? "I waited patiently for the Lord" (Ps. 40:1).

Purity of Heart, Part 1

Blessed are the pure in heart, for they will see God.
—*Matthew* 5:8 (*NIV*)

The Desert Elders often said that their quest was for the dominion of God. Then they clarified that the way to get there was purity of heart. Anything that fosters purity of heart the Desert Elders embraced. Anything that didn't they let go.[20] But, purity of heart is an imprecise objective. Who has ever seen purity of heart?

Purity of heart is a heart that's free—free from attachments and aversions. It's a heart that's free from the carrot and stick (the carrot of reward if we do right and the stick of punishment if we do wrong). When we free our minds of all attachments and sense objects in centering prayer we behold this primordial freedom. We free our minds of all images, symbols, words, and thoughts.

At this point many will say, "Why would I want to free my mind of thoughts?" "Thinking is normal. I don't have a problem." Maintenance drinkers will also say, "I only drink a certain amount each day. I don't have a problem." If this is the case, then the evidence that there's no problem is to quit. If the drinker can quit the drinks for a month with no withdrawal symptoms then there's no problem, and if the thinker can quit the thoughts periodically, then there's no problem. Yet the reality is that the maintenance drinker usually can't stop drinking and the thinker usually can't stop thinking. There is no "off" button. That's a problem.

We can only materialize an "off" button and learn how to press it if we train the mind and get support. In the case of thought, the way we eventually stop is through the practice of centering prayer or meditation—we habitually let go of strings of thought. Otherwise we're enslaved by them. Our enslavement may not be as severe as the alcoholic's enslavement to alcohol. Yet, we're enslaved nonetheless.

Without training to let go of thoughts, our minds remain compulsive and subjugated. In contrast, the pure heart is free of all cravings and compulsion. Freedom is letting go of all compulsions. The freer we are of any and all impulses, including the obsessive tapes we play over and over in our minds, the more likely we are to see God. God can't be invoked when we're distracted. Only when all preoccupations of the mind slowly fade, magic happens. Then we enter God's realm. Silence and stillness are the portals to a categorically different world. Silence and stillness are Dorothy's Land of Oz, Jack and the Beanstalk's castle in the clouds, and C. S. Lewis's hidden land of Narnia. Narnia and Oz beacon with the invitation to be still.

What ultimately distinguishes God from the world? The world is characterized by various systems of punishment and reward. The Spirit is characterized by freedom from all compulsions. This is why the way of the desert is to let go of all things that aren't God.

To habitually let go is painful. It scars the ego. When we repeatedly let go of the self-image we have propped up for years, it's a kind of dying process. We aren't in control and we don't like it. Yet, it's precisely this repeated letting go that eventually leads to God, who is beyond all names and forms, beyond affirmation and negation, beyond anything we can grasp.

Purity of Heart, Part 2

God is my shepherd, I shall not want;
God makes me lie down in green pastures,

and leads me beside still waters,
God restores my soul.
God leads me in paths of righteousness
for the sake of God's name.
Even though I walk through the valley of the shadow of death,
I fear no evil;
for you are with me;
your rod and your staff—
they comfort me.
—Psalm 23:1–4 (AIV)

"I shall not want" is the culmination of the centering prayer journey. It echoes a line found in *The Philokalia*: "I desire nothing that I don't already possess." That's contentment.

The market economy manufactures insecurity, which then can be quelled by some object that will make someone feel complete or "cool." Marketers work long hours to generate a perception that we lack something—a sense that we need this and we need that. To not need or want anything is the fulfillment of the mystic and the nightmare of the advertiser.

On the journey of faith, instead of the multiplicity of needs and desires for more food, clothes, and experiences, we let go and trust in the Shepherd who takes care of our needs. This trust is not naïve or irrational. It's trans-rational. In its mature phase, it represents a higher state of consciousness than reason can fathom. Reason is wonderful within its range of ability. It can build bridges and airplanes. Yet, reason is tied to the senses, which are terribly limited. God is perceived in the higher reaches of the mind—with the spiritual faculties,[21] which recognize untold depths beyond the senses.[22]

The Shepherd meets our spiritual need for ultimate security. When nothing more is needed or desired we're free from enslavement to the whims of culture and desire. This is homecoming—coming home to our ultimate reliance on God and the unshakable security derived from that reliance.

The Shepherd's path requires the opposite of noise: silence; the opposite of restlessness: stillness; the opposite of the crowd and shallow company: solitude; the opposite of a sated appetite: hunger; the opposite of ease: hardship. Yet paradoxically, this path of letting go leads to freedom. "God leads me beside the still waters" (Ps. 23:2). God's language, reserved for intimates, is stillness and silence.

"Still waters" lead us to communion and intimacy with God. We're not led to still waters by habitually engaging the senses. To follow God's lead toward still waters requires meeting God on God's terms. This is the most profound shift that someone can make—a shift from "this is my agenda" to "this is not about me and my agenda" (see Gal. 2:20). When all the senses and the desire for sense objects finally stills, the ego is not in control. The usual filters that distort divine union are quieted. At first, we feel our way in the dark, and the dark is unfamiliar. In time, even though it's dark (the senses are suspended), we build up a memory of the house's floor plan. We begin to navigate the hardwood floors with greater ease (see John 14:2).

"The Lord is my Shepherd." "I shall not want" sights or sounds or any other sensory gratifications. I have everything I need in stillness (Ps. 23:2), darkness, and silence. That's purity of heart.

Returning and Rest, Part 1

I will entice you into the desert and there I will speak to you tenderly in the depths of your heart.
—Hosea 2:14

Jesus frequented deserted places (Lk. 5:16, Mk. 1:35). The Greek word translated *desert* means "uninhabited," "lonely," and "no human population." The greatest gift of deserted places is the chance to be alone with God. Empty places help us shake the distractions that incessantly clutch at our sleeves. Deserted places help us to see with brilliant clarity that the enemy of the best (solitude with God) is the good (the sticky notes that populate the refrigerator door).

Conversely, the gift of solitude with God can become a source of terror. If during centering prayer there are no distractions, no thoughts, words, images, smells, sounds, sights, tastes, then what's left? Is anything left? Or is there just a great void? The courage of the mystic is to experientially explore this profound question. And the results will surprise us. When we're completely emptied of all sensory stimulation there is a subtle stirring that no words can touch, that sends shivers of joy up our spines.

When the mind and body are routinely "deprived" of sensory stimulation, what *The Philokalia* writers call "the spiritual faculties" emerge. These modes of perception beyond the senses allow us glimpses of the absolute. These glimpses intoxicate. There is a reason why the observers at the original Pentecost thought that those gathered were intoxicated (Acts 2:13). The Spirit inebriates. Yet, ironically, intoxication takes place most honestly and consistently on a meditation cushion.

The swirl of human activity and crowds can be a temporary comfort, a false security. But when we're free from the churn of human activity, God can lay bare the deepest intentions of our hearts. In the desert, we're alone with ourselves and must face the question: Who am I, really? When we retreat from human bustle we're often confronted with what we have avoided at all costs in the past.

The desert, so desolate and sparse, requires us to strip off all that's nonessential about ourselves. This terrifies us because we're deeply invested in the outer layers. We have become attached to the costume, persona, mask. God asks us to shed pretensions and to strip down to our essence like Adam and Eve in the garden (Gen. 2:25). Then we have to take a perilous and solitary journey, a journey back to the center. It's the journey of shedding layers. "[We come] to know God through the loss of all that is false about ourselves," says David Rensberger.

Returning and Rest, Part 2

For thus said the Lord GOD, THE HOLY ONE OF ISRAEL,
"In returning and rest you shall be saved;
in quietness and in trust shall be your strength."
—*Isaiah* 30:15 (RSV)

A few isolated, though intense, flashes of the spirit of understanding and
wisdom will not make a person a contemplative in the full sense of the
word; contemplative prayer is only true when it becomes more or less
habitual.[23]
—*Thomas Merton*

Contemplation isn't about a glimpse here and there. It's about a transformation of consciousness and habit. Contemplation is "returning" (Isa. 30:15) again and again day after day, year after year. In other words, transformation is characterized by repetition. There's nothing that substitutes for consistent practice.

Thomas Merton is one of my favorite spiritual writers, yet I'm baffled by the difference between our life paths. From his writing, I gather that he stumbled upon contemplation after extended periods in solitude and silence. My path, on the other hand, has been about daily disciplined practice.

Merton was a monk and I was an athlete. Perhaps this explains the difference in approach. This realization opened my mind. I used to think that contemplation required daily disciplined silences—athletic discipline. Now I realize there are many different ways to arrive at contemplation. I still maintain that Merton's path is the rarity. For the majority of seekers discipline is more effective.[24]

One of my frustrations in centering prayer circles is the lack of discipline. It seems that most often people who are perhaps more free-spirited than I are the ones who take to meditation. And when I ask them about their practice they talk about how they spontaneously enter into a "flow." They talk about how circumstances unfold organically with exquisite timing—they get lost in the moment and carried on the current. I don't doubt the sincerity of these responses and I celebrate their contemplative awareness. Yet, my practical side jumps in with, "Most of us don't have that luxury. Most of us have demanding jobs and family commitments."

If centering prayer is to get more traction in our culture, it will require discipline. Painful choices need to be made to carve out time from an already busy schedule. In time, then, disciplined silences become habitual, and the scaffolding of support groups and fierce determination can be removed. Then silence becomes a constant returning, a way of life. "Returning and rest" (Isa. 30:15). This is the habit.

Saint Gregory called the depths of contemplation "resting in God."[25] Once we have a taste of this rest, it effortlessly draws us back again and again. We become more and more intimate with our silent love because she "saves" us (Isa. 30:15). She saves us from the endless deliberations of our minds, which get tangled in knots over the quandaries of our times and the trifles of our lives. Most people never unravel the knots of their minds. Returning, quiet, and rest are our salvation because we let go of the binaries. We let go of the seesaw mind. We let go of people's reductionist labels. In that spaciousness we find ultimate Rest.

When we come out of that Rest, we can approach the quandaries of the day with more confidence and creativity. We have a greater ability to hold opposites in creative tension. We have eyes to see a way through dilemmas. When this pattern happens enough, we gain trust—trust that "a way will open." "A way will open" is a phrase uttered by Quaker elders. It means, "Okay, you have a predicament. Give it time. Have faith. By the grace of God you'll eventually see a way through." (See Ps. 27:14.)

At some unpredictable, opportune moment the knot will unravel. A consistent centering prayer practice unravels knots enough times that we know this is true. So, the quandaries that vex our colleagues and cause hand-wringing. . . . we can find a comfy place and wait it out. And, maybe in the meantime we will pick up a paint brush or a calligraphy pen and create something. When Jesus was presented with profound quandaries he doodled in the sand (John 8:6).

Questions for Reflection and Discussion

1)   Do you have any familiarity or experience with centering prayer?
2)   Do you agree that God is introverted and hidden? Why or why not?
3)   Does the metaphor of the lotus flower for the spiritual life speak to you? Why or why not?
4)   Monks in *The Philokalia* exclaim, "I desire nothing that I don't already possess." What do you make of this statement?
5)   Are you the type of contemplative who falls into contemplation naturally or do you require a daily discipline? Please explain.

CHAPTER 3

Christian Mysticism: A New Language

A religion without mystics is a philosophy.
—*Pope Francis*[26]

Intensity, immensity, intimacy—in the human, they all occur at once.
—*Matthew Fox*[27]

People have often asked or challenged me, "Why study mystics from so many centuries ago? What can they possibly have to say to us today?" It is true that early Christian mystics knew nothing about the Renaissance, the industrial and scientific revolutions, or the technological age. Yet, they knew most intimately what we postmoderns most desperately need: primordial freedom born of stillness.

The early mystics experienced awareness and divine union that eludes most people, including most Christians, today. They had holistic vision. Their educational and cultural development was occasionally (not *always*—have you met St. Augustine or St. Hildegard of Bingen?!) lacking by today's standards. Yet, their state of consciousness was timeless. There are three themes of the great mystics that I want to explore in this chapter, explaining how and why I am personally drawn to each of them:

1) Nature Mysticism
2) Still Small Voice
3) Stillness and Silence

Nature Mysticism, Part 1

God said, "Let there be light;" and there was light. And God saw that the
light was good.

    And God said, "Let there be land in the midst of the waters that separate
the waters." And God said, "Let the dry land appear." And God saw that
it was good. And God said, "Let the earth put forth vegetation." And God
saw that it was good.

    And God said, "Let there be lights in heaven to separate the day and
night." And God made the two great lights, the greater light to rule the day,
and the lesser light to rule the night. And God saw that it was good.

    And God said, "Let the waters bring forth swarms of living creatures."
And God saw that it was good.

    And God made the beasts of the earth according to their kinds and the
cattle according to their kinds, and everything that creeps upon the ground
according to its kind. And God saw that it was good.

    Then God said: "Let us make human beings in our image, after our likeness."
And God saw everything that was made and behold it was very good.
—Selections from Genesis 1

Genesis 1 is where my faith journey began. I grew up in the church.
But for me it took a long time for the Christian faith to sink in. It has
been a gradual marinating. Before Christian tradition weighed in, my
tradition was hiking in the Shenandoah mountains of Virginia. There
my faith took root. There I found language to revere my Creator. First
I fell in love with God's natural world. Then Christian faith began to
draw me in.

Adam, the youth leader in my church, took me and other high
schoolers into the backcountry. The most memorable trip was an over-
night survival hike. I don't know how Adam got away with it. With the
liability issues today, he wouldn't have gotten the green light. Anyhow,
Adam took me and five other young people to a vast expanse of private
land in Virginia. Each young person was spaced about a half mile from
the next. We were supposed to "survive" with only a canteen, a survival

knife, and a few carefully selected items that could fit into a small bag Adam provided. These meager supplies were supposed to meet all our needs, including food and shelter.

The first thing on my mind was food, so I got some fishing line from the compartment in the hilt of my survival knife and threaded a hook. Then, I found a juicy worm and dangled it in front of big fish that I could see just beneath the creek's surface. But, even after I dangled the hook in front of their snouts for much of the afternoon, the fish wouldn't bite.

Sunburned, hungry, and dejected, I began the second task: shelter. This project would be less frustrating because I'd taken a shortcut. Along with my survival knife, fishing line, and strike-anywhere matches, I had brought a small hammock. And lo and behold, in the area I was assigned there was a small bridge over a creek. What fortune. The perfect shelter. While the other survival hikers were busy constructing makeshift dwellings out of sticks, grass, and mud, all I had to do was string my hammock beneath the bridge. So clever.

Shortly after the sun set I shimmied along bridge beams and strung the hammock. Once I carefully got in, I was content. Yet, my empty stomach grumbled, so it took me a while to fall asleep. Finally, I got there, and then, in the middle of the night the unthinkable happened. I took a turn in the hammock and snap, I fell headlong into the creek. I went from warm and cozy sleep to total submersion in jolting ice cold water. Everything went in the creek: cloths, jacket, survival kit. It was the rudest awakening of my life.

But that plunge did something to me that I've never quite been able to put into words. As I came up from the creek, thrashing and sputtering, I felt more alive than I had ever felt in my life. My heart pounded wildly. Wave after wave of exhilaration electrified my body. Every ounce of my body from head to toenails was on fire. Euphoria. I experienced nature in the raw and gulped it down. That river plunge was my first religious awakening.

Somehow, the exhilaration of that experience convinced my young soul once and for all that life is good. Up to that moment some doubt remained. After that experience, I was shocked into awareness that life is more than good. It's adrenaline-charged and magnificent, a symphony of the senses.

On some level I had always known that life was good, but that experience tipped the scale. I came up from the creek gasping and shouting. I was a new boy, a new creation. I ran around hollering like the boy in Maurice Sendak's *Where the Wild Things Are*. "Yeah! Yahoo!" That plunge started my love affair with the backcountry.

Years later, when I lived in Montana, some winter nights I couldn't help myself: I had to sleep outside under the stars. I love to be in God's creation among the elements. That's part of the reason I got the minus-fifteen-degree sleeping bag that keeps mountaineers warm, even on frigid summits. What I love about the open sky for even just one night is the sense of freedom. The backcountry reminds us that our needs are simple. We need air, food, water, shelter, and warmth. These basics bring happiness. Everything else is not completely necessary . . . the car, the house, the cell phone, the credit card, the dishwasher . . . all dispensable.

Sometimes our over-taxed Internet-surfing minds need a place to go. . . . We need to feel independent . . . a reminder that all we require is air, water, food. . . . We often busy our minds thinking that we need other things. But, athletes of the soul remind us that happiness and freedom are as close as our next breath. We just get distracted by the commercial hubbub and frantic pace. If we get caught up in the race for money, prestige, and who knows what, we may forget that life is, in fact, sweet as it is. And the ingredients for happiness are God-given: the crisp air we inhale, the earth's bounty we devour, the fresh water we chug. . . .

Genesis 1 gives the resounding affirmation that creation is good. Genesis 1 repeats the phrase "God saw everything that was made and it was good" seven times. Usually the Bible repeats once for emphasis, and in some places there are two repetitions. But, Genesis 1 affirms creation is good seven times. There's no other phrase repeated so often in such short succession anywhere else in the Bible. This means the author of

Genesis emphasizes this point above all others. God's creation is good and the Author of creation is good. For the author of Genesis this is the starting point for the Bible and the life of faith.

In the awe-inspiring wilds, I began to know that I'm part of something mysterious that's much larger than myself, something magnificent and holy. I became a nature mystic.[28]

Nature Mysticism, Part 2

In November of 1991 I ventured into the North Cascade Mountains for a ten-day solo hike. I had the best waterproof backpacking gear, which made me feel invincible. I hiked in for five days and the rain never stopped. It doesn't matter how high-tech the gear . . . after four days of rain, everything, including my flesh, was drenched. I felt fine as long as I hiked, but as soon as I stopped, I was stone cold.

I nursed a hissing twig fire in the vestibule of my tent to stay warm at night. I crouched in front of the flame and fed the fire with a pile of damp sticks. After hours of this, I nodded off, my head flopped down, and I singed my hair. After two nights of this routine, out of pure exhaustion, I simply couldn't keep the fire going anymore. Then hypothermia set in. I stopped thinking clearly. I started doing crazy things, like peeling off articles of clothing. I was close to death. Another twelve hours of pouring-down November rain and I would have lost consciousness and died.

It was there at the edge, after six days of relentless November rain, that I had an unforgettable experience. The sun showed its radiant face.

That glorious morning, I experienced the sun for the first time as I never had before. Its rays of searing heat overwhelmed and pummeled my body. I've never been so happy to see the sun. As I bathed in the radiant warmth my eyes welled and tears of jubilation flowed. The clouds parted, the rain stopped, the sun shown in all its splendor. And I will never be the same again.

Like the river plunge of my youth, that morning transformed me. And on some level much deeper than hollow reasoning, I knew there was a God. I knew it in my toes and ear hairs. I took off all my clothes and laid them on a huge slab of rock by a mountain lake. I laid out my tent, socks, poly-pro underwear, Gore-Tex jacket. Then I laid out my limber naked body. The sun worked its magic. It dried everything and warmed everything. That morning the sun saved my life. I did not need to mouth the words that life is good. Every warmed cell in each of my ample limbs celebrated. As John Muir once wrote, "The sun shines not on us, but in us. The rivers flow not past, but through us, thrilling, tingling, vibrating every fiber and cell of the substance of our bodies."[29]

So, you see, my first love was God's natural world. As I meditated on the wilds and on life's intricate balance I began to know in my heart that there is a God . . . a Spirit that pervades all life . . . that subtly directs it to flourish. This knowledge gave me solidity, peace, and freedom. I return to this delicious knowledge again and again. "God saw everything that was made and indeed it was very good" (Gen. 1:31). Sometimes I need to get out into the deep backcountry, like the Beartooth Mountains in Montana or the North Cascades in Washington. It was the lure of wide-open spaces that drew me to make my home in the American West and Northwest, and to spend long periods of time in the Sonoran Desert of Arizona.

The earliest author of Genesis and the most ancient parts of the Bible speak of God's creation. And belief in a Creator is not naïve. Many respected scientists, such as mathematician Fred Hoyle, calculate that there is a mysterious sacred element at work in evolution. This mysterious element causes organisms to make quantum leaps forward in their development. Hoyle asserts that the transformative element at work in evolution defies all known laws of mathematics and physics. Evolutionary laws of probability can account for one or two catastrophic mutations in a single generation of species, but in order for us to have evolved to the stage we are now, as many as six or seven catastrophic mutations in a single generation of species was required. This is totally outside the realm of probability.[30] This incomprehensible, transcendent dynamic we call God.

Belief in a Creator is not unique to Christians. It's the basic spiritual heritage of native people everywhere. Native Americans, the Celts of Ireland and of the Rhineland in Germany, the native peoples of Africa and Asia, of the Polynesian Islands and New Zealand, and the Aboriginals of Australia all believe that the earth's source and the earth itself is sacred. Yes, "God saw everything that was made and indeed it was very good."

God's creation is sacred and is the great teacher. God's creation teaches the important lesson of extravagance. Annie Dillard writes,

> Nature is above all recklessly extravagant. Don't believe them when they tell you how economical and thrifty nature is, whose leaves return to the soil. Wouldn't it be cheaper for the Maple to leave its six million leaves on the tree in the first place? This deciduous business alone is a radical scheme, the work of a fanatically creative genius with limitless capital. Extravagance.[31]

Along with extravagance, nature teaches the interconnectedness of all things. Squirrel scat gives the exact nutrients that the tree roots need. Trees line the banks of rivers keeping erosion at bay. We share ninety-eight percent of our genes with chimpanzees. Seventy percent of our DNA we share with trees. The only difference between our blood and the chlorophyll found in plants is one molecule (chlorophyll exchanges one magnesium molecule for an iron molecule). Other great teachings of the natural world include diversity, resurrection, creativity, work, emptiness, balance, community, economy, and beauty.

The natural world was my first introduction into the Mystery we call God. The natural world is a sanctuary where God is revealed.

> What a wildly wonderful world, GOD!
> You made it all, with Wisdom at your side,
> made earth overflow with your wonderful creations.
> —Psalm 104:24 (MSG)

Still Small Voice

And he said, Go forth, and stand upon the mount before the LORD. *And, behold, the* LORD *passed by, and a great and strong wind rent the mountains, and brake in pieces the rocks before the* LORD; *but the* LORD *was not in the wind: and after the wind an earthquake; but the* LORD *was not in the earthquake: And after the earthquake a fire; but the* LORD *was not in the fire: and after the fire a still small voice. And it was so, when Elijah heard it, that he wrapped his face in his mantle, and went out, and stood in the entering in of the cave.*

—*1 Kings 19:11–13* (KJV)

Our behavior may not demonstrate it, but in the age of high-speed Internet, omnipresent iPhones, laser technology, and robots, we yearn more than ever before to connect with something primordial.

People don't need to be entertained or to draw attention to themselves through social media. We yearn most of all for connection. Connection with what's deepest and most mysterious about ourselves . . . connection with our souls. But our souls can't be mapped or pigeon-holed by the rules of science and they can't be reduced to sentimental niceties. Our souls remain fierce and elusive, bathed in ancient waters.

1 Kings 19:12 speaks to connection with the deepest aspect of ourselves—connection with our souls. None of the exploits of the prophet Elijah compare to this brief narrative. These words stand out. They mark a key insight of the Hebrew Scriptures. They're the nugget of pure gold after surrounding rocks have been sifted.

In the ninth century BC, Ahab and Jezebel come to the throne. They're devout worshipers of Baal who start to build a temple to Baal in the northern capital of Samaria. In the process of building the temple, Ahab and Jezebel sacrifice two of their sons to Baal. At that time Jezebel begins to hunt and butcher the prophets of Yahweh.

In Sinai on the mountain of God, Elijah, the last prophet of Yahweh, hides from royal assassins. There Elijah spent the night in a cave. Then the word of Yahweh came: "What are you doing here, Elijah?" Elijah

replied, "I'm full of zeal for Yahweh, because the Israelites have abandoned Your covenant, have torn down Your altars, and put Your prophets to the sword. I'm the only one left, and now they want to kill me."
Then God says, "Go out and stand on the mountain before Yahweh."

At that moment, Yahweh passed by. A mighty whirlwind split the
mountain and shattered rocks before Yahweh. But Yahweh wasn't in the
whirlwind. And after the whirlwind, an earthquake. But Yahweh wasn't
in the earthquake. And after the earthquake, fire. But Yahweh wasn't in
the fire. And after the fire a light murmur, which the King James Version
renders "a still small voice."

What does this passage tell us about Yahweh? Yahweh isn't Baal
the bull, not a storm God after all. This God created the weather, but
doesn't belong to its elements. God doesn't belong to the special effects.
As mystics have told us through the ages . . . God is in us, in the still
small voice, in the murmur of personal conscience. This passage gives
us a description of the voice that plays the central role in all biblical
narratives, and it sounds different from what we expect. In this one
episode Elijah provides a bridge for us to understand the inspiration
behind all the prophets and apostles. There is this still small voice that
speaks to us in the depths of our hearts and minds if we wait for our
disciplined silences to ripen.

God is the eternal Word spoken over the surface of the deep that
brings form to the universe. This Word shapes and molds all things.
As the Hebrew Scriptures tell us repeatedly, Yahweh is the "Lord of
Hosts," meaning the God above all other gods (Isa. 47:4). This infinite
Reality—this blessed Presence is beyond what our human minds can
imagine.

Some might argue that if we can't explain it, it doesn't exist. But
this is the poison of human pride. This is the pride that thinks the
creature's mind can probe the fathomless Mind at the source of the
exquisite atom. Philistines, Hittites, Moabites, and other ancient people
who occupied Palestine during the time of Israel thought of God as
finite. They thought of this god or that god embodied in this or that

statue. The Hebrews were the first people to conceive of the Lord of Hosts—the infinite God of all creation. They understood that God's Spirit penetrates us all but is not located in any of the particulars. In other words, God's energies penetrate all but are beyond all.

The second extraordinary insight of this passage is that God is in the still small voice, not the big loud voice. In other words, God doesn't pick the most obvious ways to communicate. As the mystics affirm, the art of listening for God requires diligence and stamina. Soon after this story in the narrative of the People of Israel, Jesus was born in an obscure village among those same people in a backwater of the Roman Empire. Why isn't God more visible, obvious, and conventional? Why wasn't Jesus the firstborn of the Roman emperor? And, why couldn't Jesus have enjoyed a life at the pinnacle of what civilization had to offer at the time? Why doesn't God just speak plainly or send angels we can recognize? The answer is that God is not in the obvious, but hidden in the still small voice.

This isn't to say that the business of finding God is a maze of smoke and mirrors. It is to say that the holy of holies has always been veiled.

St. John of the Cross, as well as one of my centering prayer's heroes, Thomas Keating, have said that "silence is God's first language and everything else is a poor translation." Some translations of our 1 Kings passage don't use the phrase "still small voice." They use "stillness" or "silence." Either way, may the still small voice come to us after the storm has passed and whisper the exquisite mysteries of God.

Stillness and Silence, Part 1

Practice stillness and know God.
—*The Philokalia* rendering of Psalm 46:10

The language of God is not auditory, yet it can be learned. Mandarin Chinese and Hindi and many other languages require that we learn a new alphabet just to form root words. So too, to learn the language of God, we have to learn an entirely different alphabet. That alphabet can be learned two ways: through stillness and silence.

David was a shepherd steeped in silence and stillness. Solitary shepherding in lonely places on hillsides, beside streams, and on long night watches gave David the Psalms. Silence and stillness clear our minds, like a pond freed of debris and disturbance. That clear water becomes transparent so we can see through it.

When we look into calm, clear water we see our own reflection. Illumined minds are mirrorlike. Whatever is in the scope of our experience in the present moment is reflected for what it is, without distortion or spin. We learn to see things as they are, not as we would like them to be. We gradually let go of filters and let the moment naturally materialize, without trying to manipulate it or sugarcoat it. We allow the naked moment to arise.

The prophets Elijah and John the Baptist spent much of their time living in solitary, as hermits. The Prophet Amos was a tender of sycamore trees. The Hebrews were nomadic and shepherding people who were familiar with hours of quiet and stillness. Out of this context arose the holy utterances that became Scripture.

"Be still and know that I am God" may be the single most potent biblical passage of Christian Mysticism. A profound rendering of this passage is found in *The Philokalia*: "Practice stillness and know God." This succinct and compelling synopsis of mysticism was so highly regarded that it was written on the entryways of monasteries throughout Eastern Orthodox and Oriental Orthodox lands.

People who live close to the land know stillness and quiet. Many spend time every day in the silence of wide-open spaces. For these people "be still and listen" is not a foreign concept or language. I've often found a quality, a presence of mind, a gentle serenity, among such people. When I think about their deep souls, rough hands, and slow strides, these words of Ralph Waldo Emerson come to mind: "Who you are speaks so loudly, I can hardly hear what you're saying."

With every fiber of their being there is a stillness that knows God—that doesn't necessarily talk about it, but simply knows. Talking about something can often diminish it.

Stillness and Silence, Part 2

Put some dirt in a glass of water and swirl it around, and then place the glass on a ledge. Eventually all the dirt particles will settle to the bottom of the glass, and the water will become clear.

The Desert Elders long ago used the dirt in the glass demonstration to illumine eternal principles. This is how our minds work. Numerous thoughts constantly swirl. Some thoughts are new and novel, others are the familiar tapes we play over and over. Yet, if we give it ample time primordial stillness abides, free of debris, free of distortions. Then clarity spontaneously arises. When we still our bodies our minds will eventually follow. If we exercise infinite patience our minds will become transparent like the clear water in the glass.

We can identify a spiritual truth by two criteria. First, it is infinitely simple. Second, it is infinitely difficult. This is the nature of stillness and silence.

Silence and stillness are infinitely simple disciplines. They are also infinitely difficult, especially in the context of our bombarded twenty-first-century minds. Habitual stillness and silence require deeper and deeper levels of surrender on our part. To let go of all agendas and settle into a deep silence is perhaps the most countercultural thing we can do. It requires trust that silence and stillness are indeed God's first language, and when we meet God on God's terms amazing things happen. What happens will not be by our design. We will not shape the experiences. This unfolding will not be according to our agenda.

Silence and stillness are a new language that takes a long time to learn, and even longer to learn if we hope to become fluent. Yet, the exquisite value of fluency is the delicious experience of primordial freedom.

Questions for Reflection and Discussion

1) Do you think nature and wilderness lend themselves to mysticism?
   Please explain.

2) "God is in the still small voice, not the big loud voice." What do
   you make of this statement?

3) If a cluttered mind has no room for God, on a scale of 1 to 5 (five
   being highest) how cluttered is your mind?

4) Have you had any "peak experience" such as the creek plunge and
   morning sunrise that are described from my life?

5) What is your experience with stillness and silence?

CHAPTER 4

Christian Mysticism: Self-emptying

He emptied himself.
—*Philippians* 2:7

We are asked to lose all, to be emptied out, in order to be
filled with the very fullness of God.
—*James Finley*[32]

Jesus the Exemplar

The Christian mystic takes as his or her starting point Jesus and the account of his forty-day fast in the Gospel of Matthew.

As soon as Jesus was baptized, he went up out of the water. At that moment heaven was opened, and he saw the Spirit of God descending like a dove and alighting on him. And a voice from heaven said, "This is my Son, whom I love, with him I am well pleased." Then Jesus was led by the Spirit into the wilderness to be tempted by the devil. After fasting forty days and forty nights, he was hungry.
—*Matthew* 3:16–4:2 (*NIV*)

Jesus fasted forty days and forty nights. Upon this Scripture, all Christian mysticism depends.

What's the big deal? Here it is: I take the forty-day fast at face value. There is no reason I shouldn't. All of the Gospels refer to it. This story is no metaphor. It is no yarn spun by the ancients. It is the stark fact of how Jesus came to his ministry. Jesus came to his ministry by way of a forty-day fast in the desert.

The only way a person can survive a forty-day fast is years of training. If you or I were to attempt a forty-day fast without training we would be hospitalized or die of toxemia. The body needs to build up to a forty-day fast. The point is that Jesus trained rigorously. Jesus was a spiritual athlete. And his forty-day test and transformation in the desert didn't occur in a vacuum. Jesus lived for 33 years and the Gospel only records two-and-a-half years of ministry. What did Jesus do in those silent years? Many speculate about Jesus's biography, but one thing seems to be clear: Jesus spent a portion of those years in ascetic practice and training.

What strengthens this understanding of Jesus's identity and roots is his relationship with John the Baptist. John was most likely from the Jewish monastic community of Qumran. Why? Because there is no way that John the Baptist could live in the desert without the support of an ascetic community, to bring him regular bread and water. The community at Qumran was within walking distance from the Jordan River where Jesus was baptized by John (Matt. 3:13).[33]

If we dig deeper, we discover that Qumran was an Essene community. The practice Essenes were most known for was the forty-day fast. This was the pinnacle of Essene ascetic practice reserved for their spiritual athletes. And the forty-day fast was not just a fast from food. Articles I've read suggest that the Essenes fasted from activity and from thoughts. The only way to survive the forty-day fast was to conserve all life energy, including the energy required to think and speak. All things, including bread, speech, and even thoughts, are relinquished in order to eliminate all distractions and commune with God.

The New Testament often records that Jesus went to lonely places and prayed. Jesus was also known to "pray all night" (Matt. 1:35, Lk. 5:16, Lk. 6:12). This is the Christian tradition's epicenter. And it's from this root that we trace the lineage of Christian mysticism through the ages. "I will allure you into the desert and console your heart," as Hosea 2:14 says.

Jesus and Solitude

As often as possible Jesus withdrew to out-of-the-way places for prayer.
—*Luke 5:16* (MSG)

When we're caught in the swirl of everyone else's agendas and projections, a fog creeps over our minds and keeps visibility shallow. But when we regularly withdraw from the crowd we attain perspective and clarity. Then we can be prophetic.

In lonely places Jesus established mystic communion with his Abba, which is the word Jesus uses for God the Father—a word that roughly translates "Daddy." That intimacy sustained him. Because of that cosmic unitive embrace (both intimate and immense) Jesus could sustain the demanding travel schedule, the copious misunderstandings of disciples, and the dissipating jags with jealous scholars and wounded souls.

Solitude and solidarity are two sides of the same coin. How can we seek genuine solidarity with another complicated soul unless we have first found comfort in our own skin? How can we know solidarity with another unless we've first peeled back the layers of our own souls and their qualitative strata of motivations?

First I must know "Amos" before I can know "You" (capital A and Y). If I only know "amos" I will only come to know "you" (lowercase a and y). Deep calls to deep (Ps. 42:7). My inherent dignity and worth confidently perceives the inherent dignity and worth in you. Thomas Merton said, "Very often it is the solitary who has the most to say; not that he uses many words, but what he says is new, substantial, and unique. He has something real to give because he himself is real."[34]

The Gospel says this, as well, about the spiritual practice of Jesus:

Very early in the morning, while it was still dark, Jesus got up, left the house and went off to a solitary place, where he prayed. Simon and his companions went to look for him, and when they found him, they exclaimed: "Everyone is looking for you."
—Mark 1:35–37 (NIV)

Jesus got up and went while it was still dark, it says. Early morning hours are powerful. My centering prayer sessions are usually more powerful at dawn. When we first wake, our minds haven't accumulated stresses from the day. The sun's rays are fresh and the day is new. In the morning, the mind is like the river at its source before it has accumulated debris downstream.

I like the Scripture's use of the word "solitary." There is a huge difference between lonely and solitary. Lonely is a fragment of a larger whole, which is lacking. Solitude is whole and feels no lack. Solitude is a blessing that comes after hard-won cultivation. Loneliness is a curse like hunger or some other privation. "Loneliness is inner emptiness. Solitude is inner fulfillment," says Richard Foster.[35]

Jesus and Asceticism

After fasting forty days and forty nights . . . Jesus was filled with the power of the Spirit.
—Matthew 4:2, Luke 4:14

Is asceticism a bad word? Maybe so, because in the popular imagination it reeks of self-flagellation, hair-shirts, and denial of the body. It must belong in the Dark Ages. But this is a twisted caricature of asceticism.

Rightly understood, asceticism liberates. Rightly understood, asceticism is freedom from compulsions. Who says that I have to compulsively eat breakfast, lunch, and dinner every day? The ascetic knows freedom from dependence on noise, incessant activity, human companionship, technology, food, sex. . . . The ascetic is not a slave to these things—and none of us should want to be a slave. An ascetic can exercise silence, stillness, solitude, fasting, abstinence, and the like. What freedom!

The ascetic is not ruled by compulsions of the senses. Life-giving asceticism opens up a new world, and I might add . . . clears a direct path to God. There's nothing wrong with food, music, technology, human companionship, activity, and sex. These are all gifts from God, all made for our enjoyment. When in balance, they contribute to an integrated and jubilant life. The problem is the addictive compulsion toward these things. The ascetic aspires to freedom from dependency on all these God-given gifts. Then and only then, can the ascetic receive the most exquisite gift. Then God's presence is no longer filtered through the senses, no longer dependent on any sense object whatsoever—this is primordial freedom. Jesus knew these profound arts of self-emptying and asceticism.

Jesus and Self-emptying

Let the same mind be in you that was in Christ Jesus, who, though he was in the form of God, did not regard equality with God as something to be exploited, but emptied himself, taking the form of a slave.
—Philippians 2:5–7a (NRSV)

This Scripture is referred to as "the kenotic verse." Kenosis is derived from the Greek word for emptiness and refers specifically to the phrase "he emptied himself" (Phil. 2:7). Kenosis is not necessarily about self-denial. The heart of kenosis is the loss of "self" altogether. If there is no "self," then there is nothing to deny. I think Paul puts it well when he says, "I [small self/false self/isolated self] no longer live, but Christ [large self/true self/connected self] lives in me" (Gal. 2:20).

Centering prayer is a process of self-emptying—the mind habitually lets go of everything that comes along the stream of consciousness. As a result of habitually letting go the mind becomes empty of words, thoughts, and images; the mind experiences a newfound spaciousness and freedom. In that space, God nudges and cajoles us. An acquisitive, cluttered mind has no room for God. First the garage must be emptied. Then there is room for the car (so my wife tells me). The mind must be cleared of distractions. Then it can receive the blessings of the Spirit and "peace that passes all understanding" (Phil. 4:7).

We can only make room for our higher power (Christ) if we clear a space. And I wish the clearing were as easy as cleaning out the garage. It's not. Self-emptying takes slow adaptation to a new way of being—a way of being that isn't dictated by desires—a way of freedom.

A novice went to see the teacher and began to chatter. As the student chattered, the teacher filled the novice's teacup. As the chatter became incessant, the teacher poured and poured until the tea ran out onto the table, then onto the floor.

The novice jumped up and cried, "What are you doing? The tea is spilling everywhere!"

The teacher replied, "This cup is like your mind. It's so full that it can't receive anything new." This is the challenge. The Gospel can only be received if our cup is empty.

If we're serious about the spiritual journey, we will empty the cup. This can be painful. The contents of the cup may represent prior knowledge that is of no use now. It requires humility to let go, then let go some more. Then you guessed it, let go some more. We let go of our preferences and our agendas. We let go of our cultural conditioning and our thoughts.

Letting go is a muscle reflex that can be exercised and toned in prayer so that it becomes more and more habitual. At first, we routinely think about whether or not we want to let go of an enticing thought process. With time, we skip the deliberations and instinctively let go.

If we believe the mystics, after the art of letting go becomes habituated, God gets to work and secretly transforms us in ways beyond our comprehension. God can only fill us when we're empty. Emptiness leads to fullness. Emptiness is the highest wisdom.

Jesus and the Cross

My old self has been crucified with Christ. It is no longer I who live, but Christ lives in me.
—*Galatians 2:20 (NLT)*

As disciples of Jesus we model his journey by "putting off the old self" (Eph. 4:22). When we put on the new self we are re-created with Christ. We are a new creation. This is an Easter Resurrection story.

Eventually the journey of self-emptying concludes with the words, "Thy will, not my will, be done" (Lk. 22:42). It is then that we can say, "It is no longer I who live, but Christ who lives in me." It is then that we don't follow the lead of our ego and its agenda. We become Christ followers. As he emptied himself we empty ourselves.

Questions for Reflection and Discussion

1) Can you see how, in your life, regular alone time/solitude might allow for greater intimacy with others?

2) Do you think that periodic abstinence from sense cravings such as noise and food could be liberating? Why or why not?

3) Is there something, someone, or some idea that you need to let go of in your life? If so, who or what? Why?

Part Two:

STRUGGLE AND HEALING

Do not reject hardship.

—MAXIMUS THE CONFESSOR

Jacob wrestled the angel. . . .

—GENESIS 32:23–31

CHAPTER 5

◆ ⎯⎯⎯⎯⎯⎯⎯⎯ ◆

Struggling for Freedom

We should be careful lest it should happen to us that while we are talking about the journey along the narrow and hard road we may actually wander onto the broad and wide highway.
—John Climacus[36]

Unexpected trials are sent by God to teach us to practice the ascetic life.
—Hesychios the Priest[37]

In *The Philokalia* Maximus the Confessor states bluntly: "Do not reject hardship."[38] And Psalm 17 reiterates, "I have kept to difficult paths" (Ps. 17:4). A consistent characteristic of integrity is the acceptance of hardship. A consistent temptation is to avoid hardships and opt for easy shortcuts.

Sometimes hardship and suffering is accepted for a greater good and sometimes it comes through folly. For example, in the parable of the Prodigal Son the father does not prevent his son from making his own mistakes and suffering as a result (Lk. 15:11–32). The father allows that space. The father understands that we learn wisdom through our own free will, struggle, and suffering.

▨ Discerning Motivations

We justify our actions by appearances; God examines our motives.
—Proverbs 21:2 (MSG)

The good person out of the good treasure of the heart produces good, and the evil person out of evil treasure produces evil. . . .
—Luke 6:45 (AIV)

Hidden motives direct our thoughts and our behavior. The heart makes life complicated, because we can never be completely sure of someone's intentions—or sometimes, even our own. Someone may do something that looks great on the surface but the intention is evil. Likewise, someone may do something that looks terrible on the surface but the intention is good. We never know because no one has ever seen a motivation.

Only God sees the motivations of our hearts. Proverbs says, "We justify our actions by appearances; God examines our motives." The heart is the center of our being because that's where our motivations originate. What we want and what we don't want begins in the heart.

In the games that the head plays with the heart, the head always plays catch-up. We prefer to believe that we first think through a course of action, launch it, and then become excited about it—in that order. More likely, our feelings get excited and push us in a certain direction first, and only when we find ourselves in the midst of the action do we begin to think about it. So the motives of the heart drive most of our actions. Later on, we start to think about it and most likely to rationalize it.

To get at underlying motivations, we can put our minds on alert to observe and review our feelings, to question our emotions. "Hmm—I'm feeling annoyed tonight. Now wait a minute. Just what or with whom am I annoyed? Maybe it's not my wife; maybe it's not my children; maybe it's not my boss who just criticized me because I botched the assignment. Maybe I'm really annoyed with myself. Because the truth (and on some level of our being we know the truth) is that I waited so long to get started on that assignment that there was no way I could have succeeded." Then we ask ourselves, "Why did I wait so long to start the assignment? The assignment must not be a priority to me. Why?"

When we carefully ask such questions we probe the heart's underlying motivations.

In Chinese wisdom there are three primal symbols of power. There's the power of the sword (the will), the jewel (wealth), and the mirror (self-knowledge). Of these three the mirror is most prized. For when we know our deepest selves—our heart and its motivations, we become wise.

Many people don't know their underlying motivations. The real reason we do what we do is hidden from ourselves. But the wise take time to listen to their hearts to decipher the real reasons why they do what they do. Jesus often says that external actions don't count to God. What counts is the internal motivations of our hearts (Mk. 12:38–40). "It is the heart that experiences God," said Blaise Pascal. To listen to and know the heart is the essence of the spiritual path.

Glimpsing Our Original Nature

At about that same time Jesus left the house and sat on the beach. In no time at all a crowd gathered along the shoreline, forcing him to get into a boat. Using the boat as a pulpit, he addressed his congregation, telling stories. "What do you make of this? A farmer planted seed. As he scattered the seed, some of it fell on the road, and birds ate it. Some fell in the gravel; it sprouted quickly but didn't put down roots, so when the sun came up it withered just as quickly. Some fell in the weeds; as it came up, it was strangled by the weeds. Some fell on good earth, and produced a harvest beyond his wildest dreams."

—*Matthew* 13:3–8 (MSG)

One of the primary dualisms of any social system, religions included, could be summarized like this:

   a) Some cabbages are better than others.
   b) All cabbages come from good seed.

Why are some cabbages better than others? It's not because some have more innate worth than others. All are created equal. The original seed is not the problem. Or, as the authors of *The Philokalia* put it, our "original nature" or "original purity" is not the problem.[39]

The problem is that pollutants stifle the budding plants, diseases injure, microbes infest, beetles eat the leaves, callous feet stomp. In some areas, the sun scorches or drought makes the plants brittle. These assailants, not the original seed, are the problem. The Sower sows good seed (Gen. 1:27). It's after the seeds are scattered that problems arise.[40]

I once knew a colorful character in Santa Cruz, California, named Nicola. She ran a small, privately funded library called the Resource Center for Nonviolence. Nicola grew up in the Hitler Youth, then escaped to the United States, denounced Nazism, and advocated nonviolence ever since.

One afternoon while we enjoyed tea together Nicola shared a defining moment. Nicola sat in church while the minister railed, "We're born in darkness, we're born in sin, we've been evil from infancy," and so on. Finally, Nicola couldn't take it anymore. She sprung to her feet, stood in the middle of the congregation, and called out in a loud voice, "I was born beautiful." Then she walked out.

The starting point for nearly everything in our lives revolves around the following question: Am I essentially good or essentially bad?

In the summer of 2001 I attended my first ten-day centering prayer retreat at Benedict's Monastery in Snowmass, Colorado. There, after days of centering prayer, I got in touch with my core goodness. It surprised me! I realized on a definitive experiential basis that I'm rooted in original blessing, not original sin. This original blessing is what writers of *The Philokalia* refer to as "original purity," "original nature," and our "pre-fallen state."[41]

At the core of our being we're rooted in Light. The historic Quakers often spoke of the "Christ Light" or "The Divine Light Within." The centering prayer community speaks of "The Divine Indwelling." Before that 2001 retreat I had heard such statements and I had read that "The dominion of God is within you" (Lk. 17:21), that "You are made in the image of God" (Gen. 1:27), that "You are God's temple" (1 Cor. 3:16). Yet, those words didn't take hold until I experienced them firsthand, and I didn't experience them firsthand until I had been steeped in tens of hours of stillness and silence.

When I work with people, sometimes I close my eyes and remind myself that underneath the layers of this person's false pretenses and dysfunction, there's that core goodness. This is true for all of us! Underneath the layers of blurred vision, abuse, addiction, childhood trauma, or neurosis there's the primal Light. Beneath the years of cultural scripting and self-centered cleaving, there is this core goodness.

We were all in touch with primordial light and freedom when we were children. Yet, people get pummeled by the years and mugged by the assailants. They lose touch with their core. That's why when the disciples start their head trips about who is the greatest disciple, Jesus places a child before them. Then he says, "The dominion of God belongs to this child" (Lk. 18:16). Why? Because the child is closer to the radiant source. We're further removed.

The child revels in the Garden of Eden. We, on the other hand, are trying to find our way back. And the way back to Eden will not be easy. The entrance is guarded by a flaming sword (Gen. 3:24). To recover our original nature will require struggle. It will require humility. . . . It will require willingness to unlearn much of what we have learned and willingness to shed layer upon layer of cultural conditioning.

▒ Chaos and the Word

In the beginning God created the heavens and the earth. Now the earth was formless and empty, darkness was over the surface of the deep, and the Spirit of God was hovering over the waters.

And God said, "Let there be light," and there was light. God saw that the light was good, and separated the light from the darkness.

—Genesis 1:1–4 (NIV)

This Genesis passage has opened a way for me to see the world. It has opened a way for me to make sense of horrors on the news, such as the slaughter of young children at Sandy Hook Elementary, and other school shootings.

Tragedy fills our world with car wrecks, broken marriages, depression, chronic illnesses such as Parkinson's and ALS, and suicide. Terrorism becomes more and more widespread, with no foreseeable end. We turn on the news and see thousands murdered in Nigeria, or children gunned down in India. We learn that scores of people have been massacred in a major European city, or a militant group in the Middle East has carried out a series of ritual murders. The list goes on. . . . It is all too much to bear.

In Genesis, the earth was formless and chaotic waters reigned. Then God said, "Let there be light," and there was light: an intelligent Word penetrated the chaos. Transforming light penetrated the void, and formless matter began to take coherent shapes.

I used to reject the horrors of this world. I used to get angry with God. . . . "God, how can You have created a world where these things happen?" But, now I accept that there's an element of chaos in this world. There's a murky, formless deep—void of reason—witnessed in Genesis. There are these turbulent waters in our lives and in the lives of those around us—storms of alcoholism, rage, fear, grief, environmental apocalypse, perpetual war, needless tragedy. Simple acknowledgment that there's a random chaotic element in the world is a great blessing. Then we no longer run from the chaos or try to explain it away.

People tend to have two polar reactions to chaos in the world. The first reaction is to try to explain it all away with some fantastic system of thought. Some people would have us think that everything is pre-ordained by God. I can't believe in a God who ordains such things as the Holocaust or the Russian labor camps under Stalin. This kind of thinking makes no sense.

There are also people who think that everything makes sense and is in fact rational if we understand laws of karma and reincarnation.

Such theological systems are extremely complex and filled with holes. I can't believe, as these systems try to prove, that we all get what we deserve—that we somehow subtly reap what we sow. This is true to some extent, but it only goes so far. What about the child dying from malnutrition in Cambodia? Did this girl do anything to deserve this suffering? What about the boy in India maimed by his parents so that he draws more money begging? Did he get what he deserved? What about the multimillionaire who does nothing to serve humanity, but instead uses all his wealth to make even more of a killing with cutthroat business practices and unethical trading? What about the kids shot on the playground at their elementary school?

The more I take a hard look at the various tragedies of our times the more I'm convinced that there's no rational explanation. There's no overarching system of thought, whether it's predestination or karma or the infinite power of God that adequately explains such phenomena.

The most satisfactory explanation of so much of the suffering in the world is that there is in fact a chaotic element at work in the world. We would like to have a system that explains this chaos away so that everything makes sense, but I don't think any system can offer this. There's a certain amount of random chance built into the universe. Chaos Theory confirms this. What Chaos Theory also confirms is that there are limits to the chaos. In other words, there is chaos, yet the chaos exists within a larger coherence and symmetry.[42]

The problem people get into when they think about suffering is that they swing to one side of the pendulum or the other. They think everything makes sense and happens for a reason. Or they think everything is a game of chance: "This world makes no sense, there is no God, and it's tossed to a random process of natural selection. We should eat, drink, and be merry, for tomorrow we die. There's nothing to take seriously, because at the root of this universe is chaos and nonsense."

The truth for me is that there is an element of chaos in life and in the universe. There is also a Word that penetrates that chaos and transforms it into something useful, intelligent, and beautiful. So, there are two aspects of our universe. There's the murky deep that's existed from the beginning of time. There's also the divine Word that divides the day and night, the ocean and dry land, and creates utility and splendor out of a formless void. This creative principle inherent to God is at work in creation and reveals more and more over time, and for Christians it culminated in the Word made flesh.

Peace accepts chaos, yet focuses on the Word, which organizes, shapes, and transforms chaos. The still small voice of God gives us power to penetrate the chaos and transform it. It allows us to see that at every moment, even when something terrible happens, there is a still small voice whispering, "You don't need to do this." "You can stop this." "You know this isn't right."

There is chaos in this world. Let's see that for what it is. But, the transforming insight is that God has the power to penetrate this deep chasm, these turbulent waters. We can't control many of the random horrors in our world and in our lives. There's no way to get rid of the murky deep altogether or to avoid all storms. But we can do our part to rid the world of poverty, ignorance, hatred, and greed. This will be a struggle because the chaos and turbulent waters give the impression that they are all-consuming. To step back and wait for a Word requires countercultural patience and vision.

It's easy to get overwhelmed and to feel that our efforts to eradicate the ocean of suffering are puny and futile. Gandhi said that to try to lessen the world's suffering often feels like trying to empty the ocean with a bucket. Yet, no matter how insignificant our efforts may feel, we push on. This work is built on the rational and harmonizing principle of the Word, which has nourished our souls from the beginning of time (John 1:1). The Word will not abandon us.[43]

An All-out Struggle for Freedom

Not only so, but we also glory in our sufferings, because we know that suffering produces perseverance; perseverance, character; and character, hope.
—Romans 5:3–4 (NIV)

A brilliant French geneticist once mixed the genes of two butterflies to create a new strain with more spectacular design and color than anyone had ever seen.[44] After much anticipation, the genetically engineered butterfly emerged from its cocoon. The lab technicians clapped and marveled. The press was notified and soon reporters and photographers loped into the lab. All eyes were on the butterfly as it skirmished with the cocoon. Soon the butterfly's skirmish became an all-out spasmodic struggle for freedom. The butterfly gathered its energy then frantically fluttered and convulsed. Then it rested and tried again, losing energy each time.

The drawn-out struggle seemed futile. Something had to be done. "Surely some help to free the butterfly from the cocoon won't do any harm," the geneticist thought. So, with his carefully poised scalpel he made two small incisions between the wings and the cocoon. The butterfly was finally free. Everyone cheered.

After two minutes the room hushed. But again the butterfly attempted to fly to no avail. The geneticist again tried to assist its flight. He gently nudged it off the edge of a short table. It flopped to the ground.

This engineered butterfly failed to fly because its struggle was cut short. What the scientist failed to appreciate was that only a full six hours of death-defying struggle can prepare any newly formed butterfly body and wings for flight. Anything less won't do.

Similarly, struggle and suffering prepares us for transformation. The caterpillar only obtains functional wings through protracted and profound struggle. So too, we can't cut our process short. We can't come in with a scalpel and cut the butterfly free. We can't preempt our process toward freedom.

Questions for Reflection and Discussion

1) Do you think we are essentially good or essentially bad (original blessing or original sin)? Please explain.

2) Have you ever had a definitive experience of your core goodness? Please explain.

3) Try and recall an experience in your life when you really suffered. Recount what you learned from it.

◆ ——————— ◆

CHAPTER 6

Facing Our Fears

His heart whispered, "Be aware of the place where you are brought
to tears. That's where I am, and that's where your treasure is."
—Paulo Coelho[45]

God will not look you over for medals, degrees,
or diplomas—but for scars.
—Elbert Hubbard[46]

Without intimate knowledge of our wounds, we lack the insight to heal others.

Nothing characterizes our experience of life more honestly and comprehensively than our experience of suffering, together with our habit of making each other suffer. Human history, at least for the period of time for which we have written records, has been a history of suffering.

Even the "great" events and monuments of history have a shadow side. The great pyramids of Egypt, for instance, were built on the suffering of slaves who died by the thousands doing the work. The New World of the Americas was built on the genocide of Native American peoples. As many as one hundred million Native American Indians were killed by guns, smallpox blankets, displacement, and disease. Our consciences also compel us to recall the humiliation and agony of African slaves. According to PBS 12.5 million slaves were forced to row their sardine-can prison boats across the Atlantic and dropped dead by the thousands along the way. Due to the horrible conditions, an estimated 1.8 million enslaved people died.[47]

The unwritten story of the Industrial Revolution was the pain and deprivation of the workers in the new factories and mines, and of their families. The history of South Africa until recently has been largely a story of unbearable racial humiliation and hardship.

In some areas of life there's less suffering today than in the past, in other areas there's much more. One area of life today where suffering is worse today than in the past is the number of people who live in dire poverty and misery—a billion more than in former generations. The first obvious consequence of the worldwide population explosion is more suffering for more people. I remember a child I encountered in Wobulenzi, Uganda, in East Africa, who had a bloated stomach. Flies buzzed around his head and tears streamed down his cheeks. I thought to myself, "Why was I born a middle-class American and this child was born into hunger and poverty?"

On another occasion, I visited Babi Yar in Ukraine, a notorious site of Nazi massacres. On September 29th and 30th of 1941 nearly thirty-four thousand Jews were gunned down at Babi Yar. I remember the terrible silence as I stood in that place. I've also visited Gettysburg battlefield in Pennsylvania, where a haunting silence permeated the grounds—a deep sadness hard to shake.

Why do I bring up these terrible monuments? Because there is beauty, albeit a horrible beauty, in acknowledging what's true. There's beauty in facing reality in its stark contrasts. A Christian mystic needs to face reality. She accepts things as they are, not as she would like them to be. Then, an opening of the heart happens. Our tears and wounds initiate us into our common humanity and enable healing arts.

"Jesus wept," we read in John chapter 11, and this describes how God responds to the immensity of human suffering. God responds by suffering in solidarity with us. We're not alone on this human journey—God is with us. When Jews were gunned down at Babi Yar, God was gunned down. When soldiers were maimed for life at Gettysburg, God was maimed. When hungry and disheveled refugees stream out of Syria, Somalia, and the Ukraine, God is displaced (Matt. 25:40). Jesus, "the man of sorrows" (Isa. 53:3), was enmeshed in our human condition. He suffered—and suffers—with us.

Tears

As I've gotten to know people as a minister, I've come to realize that we all have issues in our families—addiction, abuse, child molestation, mental illness, a nervous breakdown. We all have issues of one kind or another.

The ordained Presbyterian minister Mr. Rogers (Fred Rogers) once said, "We can get through anything we can talk about. And we can talk about anything." We can't get into adulthood without scars. We may try to hide our scars or put on airs. But, in some way we're all broken. And the first step toward healing is truth-telling.[48] We are called to bear one another's burdens in an appropriate setting. All of us, in the form of a confessor, therapist, or trusted friend, need someone we can be real with—someone in whom we can confide, who welcomes and accepts tears.

To avoid letting things fester we can keep a journal and get real with ourselves. Before we can find a trusted person to talk to, we trust that we can open our wounds to the light and attempt to heal them with a pen. Journaling is powerful therapy. We can sift through our reality, as it was and is. This is the essential preliminary for deepening spirituality, silent prayer, and meditation. Reflection, honesty, and acceptance heal. First, we acknowledge and lance the wounds. Then, they begin to rectify. First, we are honest with ourselves, then with another.

Frailties and Imperfections

He told them still another parable: "The dominion of heaven is like yeast that a woman took and mixed into about sixty pounds of flour until it worked all through the dough."
—Matthew 13:33 (NIV)

When Jesus talked about God he used everyday circumstances with which people were familiar. He used down-to-earth examples from everyday life. He kept his message accessible and elegant in its simplicity.

In the ancient Israelite world, leaven (today's yeast), was a symbol of corruption. Modern English usage has given it a positive connotation. But for the people of Israel, leaven symbolized the unholy, tainted, and twisted. Unleavened bread was the proper symbol of holiness and sanctity because of the absence of leaven. Leaven was a symbol of corruption because in ancient times to make leaven, a piece of bread was placed in a dark damp room until it rotted and stank.

Another significant detail is that the woman kneads three measures of flour. This is a huge amount of flour that could feed more than fifty people. So leaven, an archetypal symbol of corruption, is kneaded throughout three measures of flour. This is upside-down.

Jesus turns everything upside-down. For instance, just as the ancient Israelites thought leaven was dirty, maybe we think the compost bin is filthy. It stinks and it's full of mites, worms, and maggots. Yet, if we reflect deeply, we realize that it's in fact magnificent. The compost bin makes soil rich in nutrients so that it can bring new life. God can use the undesirable, or the unexpected, for good in our lives. God can turn everything around.

In Jesus's time people thought that the dominion of God was about the ultimate triumph of God in the world. The ancient Israelites heard about holy visions of long, flowing, white robes, dazzling light, amazing temples, and hallowed angels.

The realm of God, as Jesus taught it, is quite different. In the life of Jesus, God does not intervene with a pillar of cloud and fire (Exod. 13:21)

or with a chariot (2 Kgs. 2:11). In Jesus's stories God isn't found in mirac-
ulous occurrences from another world. God can be found in this world
we inhabit. This was a revolutionary shift.

Jesus's parables suggest that the solution is not to get away from our
problems, but to realize that God is totally present and supports us in
the midst of them. Jesus's parables suggest that to get away from the
stink is not the goal. The stenches we resist can catapult our transformation! "You mean God is even in this?" Yes.

People I know who have suffered have depth and wisdom. Of
course, we don't wish for anyone to suffer. Yet, when we suffer we learn
the essential lesson: let go. A decent definition of suffering is "to lose all
control." At first, we resist this. Then, in time, we allow ourselves to be
carried in the storm. And control is no longer a requirement. In those
storms we trust a hidden Presence that never leaves our side and that
will even be there at the time of death (the ultimate loss of control).
If we loosen our grip now, we'll be prepared for the free fall that is to
come.

Suffering is the transformative legacy of the cross. If even the most
terrifying Roman symbol of torture can be transformed, then any rot or
terror can be transformed. The rot is not wiped out or eliminated; it's a
catalyst for change. The most vivid example of this is that through Jesus
God doesn't destroy death, but joins us in death.

In the compost piles of life God is most present. In countercultural stillness we begin to understand. In the most horrible chapters
of our lives we finally learn to rely completely on God. Our ego loses
control and consequently no longer needs to be in control. Then we
wholeheartedly rely on our higher power and eventually life becomes
fluid and joy-filled. Jesus sanctifies the outcasts and whatever is outcast
within us. Jesus says, "Let me in even there, where it's rotting, where it
hurts the most."

What idea of God's realm emerges as we listen to the parable of
the leaven? It's that the leaven, compost pile, pain, doubts, fears are
not always replaced by unleavened bread, holiness, joy, clear thoughts.

Daily problems are not normally changed by divine intervention that we can see or feel. Our hope is to trust God in the everydayness with its recurrent trips to nowhere; in the midst of the recycled temptations; in the midst of our frailties, imperfections, bald spots, insecurities. Even in the darkest, dankest room where the bread is rotting: God.

The woman in the parable kneads the leaven through three measures of flour. So too, God can knead and infuse every cell of our anatomy and every aspect of our lives.

Facing Our Fears

We . . . glory in our sufferings, because we know that suffering produces perseverance; perseverance, character; and character, hope. And hope does not put us to shame, because God's love has been poured out into our hearts through the Holy Spirit, who has been given to us.
—Romans 5:3–5 (NIV)

Criminals are pushed into prison cells. The sick are tucked away in hospitals. People with memory loss loiter on Alzheimer's wards. The severely mentally ill are confined to psychiatric wards. Rabid dogs are contained at animal control centers. Government messes are covered up by the CIA. All the horrific stuff is out of sight, out of mind.

Parents instinctually shelter their children from harsh realities. Fairytales and Disneyland have mass appeal because they're far removed from the messiness of real life. Religion often serves the same purpose—to shelter us from unwanted complexity. The real world is too complicated and messy to wrap our minds around. So, our belief system becomes a safe haven, where the gray areas are swept away—where we're comforted by fanciful notions of black and white and right and wrong, where the bad guys wear black hats.

Television and movies offer a similar tonic. Where are the obese people, except on the most awful sort of "reality TV" shows? Where is the seventeen-year-old dying of leukemia? Where's the child suffering from shaken-baby syndrome who requires constant care around the clock? Where's the AIDS victim?

Jesus's day was no different. The leper wasn't allowed near the city. The prostitute was cast out of the neighborhood. The tax collector (extortionist) was forbidden from respectable homes. Out of sight, out of mind.

We want to believe the fairytale. We want to believe the dragon will be slain and everyone will live happily ever after. But what about old age, disease, random acts of violence, and death? Again, the instinct is to tuck it away somewhere out of site. Calamity, suffering, and the cross will never be popular. It's human nature to look the other way. Our society protects us from calamity. From a young age we're sheltered from what goes terribly wrong. So, when calamity strikes we're stunned. We can't believe it happened to us.

After eighteen years of ministry I'm no longer surprised when calamities strike. My eyes have opened. I see that adversity is part of everyone's life—that calamity will come sooner or later, often repeatedly. A big part of ministry is facing fears and trying to help others come to terms with adversity.

Just the other day I talked to a woman named Jane who recently suffered from cancer. She survived the rounds of chemotherapy and radiation and is now in remission. One would think that the normal response to such a situation would be "Wow, I'm glad that's over. Now let's not talk about it again." But Jane's response to her bout with cancer surprised me. She brought it up, then said "My cancer was a gift." I said, "Come again?" She continued, "As a result of the cancer I live my life differently. I see every day for what it is: a precious gift." "Time is priceless; every hour is a sacrament." Jane started out as a cancer patient. She ended up a mystic.

Give Thanks in All Things

Rejoice always, pray without ceasing, in everything give thanks, for this is the will of God in Christ Jesus for you.
—*1 Thessalonians 5:16–18 (NKJV)*

Paul's letter to the Thessalonians pushes "giving thanks" beyond typical notions. Paul says, "In everything give thanks." We might ask: *"Everything?* Did I hear that right?" We can't in our right minds give thanks for disasters. And we can't reasonably give thanks for the emotional paper cuts, sharp pains, and enduring scar tissue. But Paul asks us to go beyond normal thanksgiving—beyond counting our blessings. We do give thanks for our blessings. Yet we also count our wounds and adversities and give thanks.

How can we give thanks in all things? One way is to make the distinction to give thanks *"in* all circumstances," not *"for* all circumstances. . . ." We don't give thanks for the horrors of our times. Yet, faith can give us the ability to give thanks in the middle of terrible circumstances.

One Veterans Day I listened to a World War II veteran on the radio talk about adversity when he was a prisoner of war. He went without food for a week or ten days at a time and was often so hungry he wished that he could rummage through a restaurant dumpster. On a march to a concentration camp half the soldiers in his platoon died. He and his fellow soldiers bartered in rubber and leather for shoe repair. Shoes meant the difference between surviving a march or not. For months they were forced to dig all day. If a prisoner slowed down, he was prodded with a bayonet. Prisoners worked six days a week, twelve hours a day. Many of his friends died of exhaustion.

One day the man started to draw. In time, he searched for anything to draw on. Bits of charcoal became his pencils. Drawing kept him alive.

When he got back to the United States he spent a year in the hospital. The doctor said his heart had enlarged to twice its size as a result of poor nutrition and too much hard labor.

What amazed me was the veteran's comment that he would do it all again. What? He explained that the reason he would do it all over again was that he was a different person now. The wounds of brutal imprisonment gave him renewed appreciation for the countless garden-variety blessings of everyday life. He also became a success in business. He said that most of the people he knew who survived the concentration camps went on to success in their personal and professional lives. Adversity gave them perspective and tenacity. Nothing seemed hard compared to the hardships of the camps. And the suffering they endured made them empathetic.

The lyrics of an old Gospel spiritual say, "If it doesn't break me, it will just make me stronger." Faith tested by adversity can face two shipwrecks, a stoning, five imprisonments, and five beatings to the edge of death (forty lashings minus 1), and three beatings with rods (see St. Paul in 2 Corinthians 11!). Not only does Paul endure all this and keep going . . . but the extraordinary thing is that he faces it all with joy! Paul is the embodiment of "in everything give thanks."

Philippians is my favorite Pauline letter because it's the most joyful. There's no earthly reason why Paul should be joyful. The church is persecuted, he has suffered numerous privations, and he is in prison. Yet, he's joyful. This means that his joy is not dependent on outward circumstances or on the fulfillment or deprivation of the senses. His joy is based on abiding peace—profound, stable, and a support in any and all circumstances. This joy is not dependent on externals. It's an internal groundwater that constantly flows beneath. No matter what goes on above ground it keeps flowing. This flow makes Paul genuinely thankful, even exuberant, in every circumstance.

Our faith promises us that when we suffer—there's no getting around that—we'll be able to endure it and eventually transform it. And when our faith is mature we can even suffer with joy, as paradoxical and strange as that may seem.

Questions for Reflection and Discussion

1) "Nothing characterizes our experience of life more honestly and comprehensively than our experience of suffering." Do you agree? Why or why not?

2) "There is beauty in facing reality in all of its stark contrasts." Do you agree? Why or why not?

3) "Suffering is a powerful catalyst for transformation." Do you agree? Why or why not?

4) Is there someone you can talk to in confidence about your scars? If so, who?

CHAPTER 7

◆ ──────── ◆

Birth of the True Self

You must lose yourself to find yourself.
—Jesus (paraphrase of Matt. 16:25)

I will give you the treasures of darkness and riches hidden
in secret places, so that you may know that it is I, the Lord,
the God of Israel, who calls you by your name. . . . You shall
be called by a new name that the mouth of the Lord will give.
—the prophet Isaiah (Isa. 45:3, 62:2)

Unlike physical birth, spiritual transformation is not a one-time thing. As Thomas Keating has stated and re-stated, "The Transforming Union is the restructuring of consciousness, not just an experience, or set of experiences."[49] I will try to briefly and succinctly lay out some of these important transforming experiences in this chapter.

God Anoints Wildcards

When they arrived, Samuel took one look at Eliab and thought, "Here he is! God's anointed."

But God told Samuel, "Looks aren't everything. Don't be impressed with his looks and stature. I've already eliminated him. God judges people differently than humans do. Men and women look at the face; GOD looks into the heart."

Jesse then called up Abinadab and presented him to Samuel. Samuel said, "This man isn't GOD's choice either."

> *Next Jesse presented Shammah. Samuel said, "No, this man isn't either."*
>
> *Jesse presented his seven sons to Samuel. Samuel was blunt with Jesse, "GOD hasn't chosen any of these."*
>
> *Then he asked Jesse, "Is this it? Are there no more sons?"*
>
> *"Well, yes, there's the runt. But he's out tending the sheep."*
>
> *Samuel ordered Jesse, "Go get him. We're not moving from this spot until he's here."*
>
> *Jesse sent for him. He was brought in, the very picture of health— bright-eyed, good-looking.*
>
> *GOD said, "Up on your feet. Anoint him. This is the one."*
>
> *Samuel took his flask of oil and anointed him, with his brothers standing around watching. The Spirit of GOD entered David like a rush of wind, God vitally empowering him for the rest of his life.*
>
> —1 Samuel 16:6–13 (MSG)

The anointing of God's sovereign is a vital memory in the life of ancient Israel. What jumps out in this story is the total longshot God chooses for king. How on earth can David be chosen as leader? David is the youngest son of Jesse, who belongs to the smallest clan of the smallest tribe of Israel. David wasn't even allowed to come to the ritual sacrifice that Samuel performed. He was left out in the fields to tend the family's sheep.

Samuel asks Jesse's sons to line up, and what a sight. These are the most impressive men the country can offer. These are starters for the college wrestling team, homecoming kings. When Samuel saw these guys, his reaction was similar to: Wow, now I know why God sent me to Jesse's sons. These guys have everything it takes: strong, bright, sturdy, and stately. I'm sure to find Israel's sovereign here.

Then, one by one they're all passed over! "Surely, Lord, this must be the one," Samuel thinks. "No." "Now, surely Lord this is the one." "No." This happens seven times. . . . No, no, and no. "Something must be wrong here," Samuel says to himself. "How can God pass up each and every one of these studs?" It's like being a recruiter for the University of

Arizona basketball team. You have seven all-Americans in front of you to choose from. And the owner of the team says, "No, none of them will do." Then the owner says, "Hey, you see that scrawny kid cleaning out the Gatorade jugs over in the corner—he's the one I want."

The recruiter thinks to himself that the owner is crazy. Samuel asks Jesse, "Are these in fact all your sons?" "No," Jesse answers, "my youngest is over on Sheep Dip Road. He's dipping sheep right now, he's drenched in chemicals, and he's been out on the open range for days, so he smells." Samuel says, "Great, please send for him. I'll wait here for as long as necessary." So, Samuel waits in stillness and anticipation. He puts his agenda on hold and simply waits.

How can God ignore the outward signs that we rely on and pick someone so unlikely? How could God entrust Israel's future to a boy, untested, short, awkward, and dirty? Earlier, how could God have chosen Moses, an orphan and a murderer with a speech impediment (see Exod. 4:10)? How could God have chosen Abraham and Sarah to build a nation, when Sarah was beyond child-bearing age (see Gen. 18:11)? Then, later, how or why would God choose Nazareth as the place from which something noteworthy would take place (see John 1:46)? How can God choose a peasant girl to be an essential part of God's redemption (Lk. 1:31)?

What kind of God is this? Sometimes God can seem totally irrational. Why did God choose David, a raggedy, untried shepherd boy?

The great mystery we call God uses the most unlikely people because doing so shows us that we can't do everything on our own. Our success is not about us, our qualifications, our know-how. When we rely on ourselves we're limited. We may have the gifts that the world values, but we're still inept. On the other hand, we may completely lack what the world values, yet God can use even cheap simple clay to make amazing pots. What matters most is the skill of the Potter.

God alone can provide, in spite of our glaring limitations. This is the beginning of mature faith. The Bible tells us over and over—trust God. This is the beginning of wisdom (Prov. 1:7 and 9:10, Ps. 111:10). The

Bible is riddled with people who trusted in their own abilities and failed (1 Sam. 15, Esther 4). Scripture is also filled with the most unlikely souls, who trust God and succeed.

We tend to put our trust in our own rational minds. We evaluate people based on reason and the world's standards. We get swayed by a person's image. But God sees beyond image to the intentions of the heart (see 1 Sam. 16:7). God alone knows what's best. God can bring together numerous factors outside of our control to unlock doors from the inside. When we strive and drive, control, and micro-manage, projects are doomed. On the other hand, when our intentions are genuine and not about self-aggrandizement and personal agenda, things just start to happen, and we're wise to get out of the way. We do our part, but make no mistake that it's the Spirit at work here, not the designs and manipulations of my ego.

The Holy Spirit says, "Samuel, get out of the way and trust. My ways are not your ways (Isa. 55:8). My designs hold together every atom, sparrow, family, and community. And yes, my designs will bring unlikely leadership to these scattered tribes and make them great."

Why is this a mystical passage? Because Samuel let go of what he knew and submitted to an infinitely more intelligent, albeit unpredictable, higher power. To tune into our higher power, like Samuel, we silence everything we know. Then we can encounter the mystery of God, who blesses the most unlikely characters.

David is unlikely, but he is God's pick nonetheless. The cross is an improbable path for the Messiah. We declare that the Messiah should journey to a throne, not a cross. But, Isaiah declares, "God's ways are not our ways" (Isa. 55:8).

People trust God as long as they're in control. Then, as soon as they lose control, they lose faith. This kind of faith bullies God to conform to our plans. God becomes the ultimate spotter: "God is on my side." This statement is the death of humility and the beginning of preparation of armaments for war. But Samuel models mature faith as he lets go of his need to control and simply trusts God against his better judgment. He sets aside his analytical mind's need to scan every angle. He lets go and enters into a higher mind, a new mind, an intuitive mind.

We want to rely on ourselves, appearances, the world's standards of success. It's challenging to trust a God who's beyond understanding. It's difficult to trust in a God who picks misfits and oddballs to be emissaries (Judg. 7:5–7).

Samuel thought he knew what was best for Israel, but he had to let go of his cultural scripting and make way for a counter-intuitive reality. Samuel was prophetic because he courageously leaped into the unknown Mystery.

This Scripture isn't just about trusting God's selection of an unlikely, scrappy shepherd. It's about trusting God in the unlikely circumstances of our lives. No matter the circumstances, God can use them for good (Rom. 8:28). We might think to ourselves, "Even *this* can be used for a higher purpose?!" The answer is yes.

God can use an untested runt to accomplish God's purpose. God can even use unlikely people like you and me. In fact, the Bible indicates that the unlikely wildcards are God's preferred servants. God's calling of wildcards is a grace. And these wildcards know that grace instinctively, so they effortlessly communicate it to others.

Love Yourself in Your Uniqueness

One of the teachers of the law came and heard them debating. Noticing that Jesus had given them a good answer, he asked him, "Of all the commandments, which is the most important?"

"The most important one," answered Jesus, "is this: 'Hear, O Israel: The Lord our God, the Lord is one. Love the Lord your God with all your heart and with all your soul and with all your mind and with all your strength.' The second is this: 'Love your neighbor as yourself.' There is no commandment greater than these."[50]

—Mark 12:28–31 (NIV)

If your experience mirrors mine, you have heard many, many messages on the love of God and neighbor. But what's usually missing, and what completes the epigram, is the notion of loving yourself. This third leg is often neglected. Yet, without the third leg the stool can't stand.

Unless we're true to ourselves, hold our heads up and respect ourselves, love ourselves, how can we expect to love others? Jesus's greatest commandment is "love your neighbor as yourself." Yourself is part of the equation. Respect starts with yourself. Eleanor Roosevelt said, "No one can make you feel inferior without your consent." Dignity or inferiority start within. And from there they radiate out, respecting and loving others, or alternatively, belittling self and others.

Our society has become dominated by media ideals of beauty and success. People who don't live up to the ideals often feel some form of self-hatred. Children in our competitive society often get the message that they're not adequate—that they're not worthy of love. They are! This is the essence of the Gospel. We can't serve others unless we take good care of ourselves in our uniqueness. We can't listen to others until we've taken the time to listen to the deep stirrings of our own souls—to our unique dreams. We can't attend to others' needs unless we first take care of ourselves.

Each of the three legs of the stool could take up several books. They're basic anchors of faith: love God, love your neighbor, and love yourself. Each is indispensable and complements the other. We can't serve our neighbors without loving ourselves or we'll burn out. We can't truly love ourselves without serving our neighbors, because personal fulfillment and joy are rooted in service. Each leg supports the others. "Love your unique self" completes the epigram.

Realize Your True Beauty

You have searched me, LORD, and you know me.
—Psalm 139:1 (NIV)

The deepest aspect of ourselves is concealed in "the secret place of the Most High" (Ps. 91:1). The only one who can reveal this mysterious and luminous core of our being is God. Our hidden nature in God is not found on the basis of merit. There's nothing we can ever do or accomplish or receive that will reveal this gift. God alone is the mysterious midwife.

We're deceived as long as we strive to know ourselves, as if we can penetrate the depths with our reasoning minds and topographical maps. Ultimately our striving is futile. It is God who pulls away the veil in a series of flashes. And when our radiant identity knit together by God dawns we begin to be who we were created to be. As Thomas Merton once said: "The secret of my full identity is hidden in God. God alone can make me who I am, or rather who I will be when at last I fully begin to be. . . . The way of doing it is a secret I can learn from no one else but God."[51]

After years of disciplined silences, or by some fluke, God lavishes love on the mystic, not because of anything the mystic has done, but because of who God is (1 John 4:8). There's nothing we can do or not do that warrants God's love. God's love tells us, once and for all, that we're beautiful.

What worse fate can a branch have than to be cut off from the Vine? "I am the Vine and you are the branches," Jesus said in John chapter fifteen. When we're connected to the Vine, abundant life flows through us. When we're disconnected, our egocentric efforts will give unfortunate results. Only when we're connected can God birth a new mind, a new abundance, that forgives the wounds and weeps tears of freedom (something the puny ego can't do). Then, healing compassion experienced in prayer, and mediated by Jesus, is unlimited. This vast expanse invites intimacy and homecoming. We often mistakenly look for this kind of intimacy in other human beings, who can never deliver. People can never fill the God-shaped-hole.

The true self, which God "knit together in our mother's womb" (Ps. 139:13) is indestructible. It's the still water at the ocean's depths, unmoved by the squall that rages on the surface. The waves on the surface come and go. The water on the ocean floor is still, immortal, sublime.

Where can I go from your Spirit? Where can I flee from your presence? If I settle on the far side of the sea, even there your hand will guide me. . . . (Ps. 139:7, 9–10, NIV)

Wrestle the Angel

After he had sent them across the stream, he sent over all his possessions. So Jacob was left alone, and a man wrestled with him till daybreak. When the man saw that he could not overpower him, he touched the socket of Jacob's hip so that his hip was wrenched as he wrestled with the man. Then the man said, "Let me go, for it is daybreak."

But Jacob replied, "I will not let you go unless you bless me."

The man asked him, "What is your name?"

"Jacob," he answered.

Then the man said, "Your name will no longer be Jacob, but Israel, because you have struggled with God and with humans and have overcome."

Jacob said, "Please tell me your name." .

But he replied, "Why do you ask my name?" Then he blessed him there.

So Jacob called the place Peniel, saying, "It is because I saw God face to face, and yet my life was spared."

The sun rose above him as he passed Peniel, and he was limping because of his hip.

—Genesis 32:23–31 (NIV)

In ancient times, a name was much more than a label of identification. One's name held the essence of one's personality. Know the name and you have the secret of the person. In his struggle with the angel, Jacob asks, "Tell me, I pray, your name." Jacob's question reveals the power of knowing a name. If Jacob discovers the name, he will have power over the angel. So, the angel refuses to give it. In the same way, when Moses asks God's name, God answers, "I AM WHO I AM" (Exod. 3:14, NIV). In other words, God says, "I'm beyond your control. I can't be named. I will always remain mysterious, beyond your inventions, letters, names, and categories."

Naming is powerful. In philosophy before we can proceed, we begin with definitions of terms. So too in the spiritual struggle, we begin with a name.

Abram risked everything, left behind all that was familiar. He too didn't know his real name. After Abram became God's faithful servant he received his God-given name: Abraham (Gen. 17:5). Sarai became Sarah (Gen. 17:15). Their true selves were born, which necessitates new names. Abram means "high father or leader" and Abraham means "very high father" or "exalted father." So Abram went from a leader of his clan to a leader of a people or nation. The name Sarai means "princess" in Hebrew. The word Sarah is a stronger form of the Hebrew root, which not only means "princess" but can also mean "Queen."

Abraham and Sarah went from their family-given names to their God-given names. They went from limited self-worth to beholding their God-given beauty. They saw that they were beautiful in God's eyes and that God had a vision for them beyond what they originally comprehended.

Before that night when Jacob wrestled with the angel, he seemed to love no one but himself. Finally, at the crossing of the Jabbok, Jacob's love extends to his family, and he identifies not only with his wife, but with his family. This isn't your average family. Jacob and Rebecca and Leah's offspring form the twelve tribes of Israel. Jacob is not just Israel by name. He and his family *are* the state of Israel!

He may have thought, *Here I thought my whole life that I was a self-centered schemer named Jacob. Now, I realize that I am a nation—a portion of God's glory.* Jacob couldn't come to this realization of his new name and his true self on his own. The angel was his midwife. Could it be that none of us knows our God-given name and true identity until we struggle for our lives in the shadows? After we emerge from the midnight struggle, we discover our God-given name—we glimpse our height and depth. God gives us a name that goes beyond family of origin. God gives us flashes of our eternal soul. God births our true self.

Fr. Gregory Boyle's book *Tattoos on the Heart* is about life among gang members in Los Angeles. Wedged in there is an amazing story about one gang member who goes to see Fr. Gregory for counseling. The priest asks the gang member, "What's your name?" "Sniper," sneers the gang member. Then, Fr. Gregory replies in the gang vernacular, saying essentially, that isn't what your mother called you. This breaks down the gang member's defenses. He replies that his homies call him "Cabrón." Cabrón means "bastard" in Spanish. Fr. Gregory replies that he needs a serious answer. He's trying to fill out a birth certificate for him.

Finally, the gang member says "Gonzales." Fr. Gregory responds, saying that that sounds like a last name. Then, more vulnerable, the gang member says that his mother named him "Napoleon." That's what she called him when she was angry with him, the man explains. Fr. Gregory asks him what she called him when she was happy to see him. At that point the gang member becomes still and quiet. "I watch him go to some far, distant place—a location he has not visited in some time," writes Fr. Gregory.[52] "Napito," the man finally says.

We all want to be called what mom called us when she was happy to see us. When we make the journey to the center, we find our name hidden in God. Like the gang member, we move through the layers of our false self with their various names, to our original self in the arms of our Abba.

When Jacob wrestles the angel he comes away with a limp. This detail is key. Before we can emerge into a larger stream of life that God has planned for us, there's an involuntary wounding or dying. This is true of tribal initiation rites. First the boy dies. Then the courageous warrior is born. First the girl dies. Then the powerful woman is born.

Our life's greatest mission comes out of our woundedness. It's precisely where we've been wounded in life that our true name is born.

To know our true name we wrestle in the shadowlands. We come to terms with the shape and history of our wound.

When we know ourselves—when we come to terms with what we hide, fear, suppress, and deny about ourselves, then we are ready for our new name. Then our true self can be born. When we wrestle the angel and hold nothing back, when we feel the panic, clutch of death, taste of oblivion, a doorway to wholeness opens. The angel will silence the evasions and lies. The angel will whisper something like, "You're a child of God. . . . Your name is no longer Jacob. It is Israel. . . ." "Your name is no longer Sniper. It is Napito." "Your name is no longer Sarai. It is Sarah." "Your name is no longer Abram. It is Abraham." "Your name is no longer violent Saul. It is beloved Paul" (see Acts 13).

The spiritual life is a colossal reorientation, where our self-seeking programs are no longer at the center. This radical reorientation doesn't come easily or willingly. It's an all-out struggle, and we emerge, if at all, with a limp. What does it mean when the angel blesses Jacob with his God-given name—when the angel says, "You are a child of God"? When we know our true name we no longer get sucked into our emotional dramas. We don't take ourselves so seriously. We no longer focus on me, myself, and I.

When I'm a child of God I no longer identify with my petty insecurities and narcissism. Wrestling the angel gives us new depth and vision. We won't get duped by liars who call us by derisive and diminishing names. We no longer succumb to self-deprecating thoughts, because we've seen ourselves shining in that brilliant Light that shone at the dawn of time. That brilliant Light will welcome us at the end. That ancient Light knows our luminous name; it knows our true self. That magnificent Light surprised the disciples on Mount Tabor (Lk. 9:28–36).

Our God-given name is not one we dream up for ourselves. It's one that God gives us: "Unless the LORD builds the house, the builders labor in vain" (Ps. 127:1). Unless the angel gives us our name we remain in darkness.

Lose Yourself

Those who want to save their life will lose it, and those who lose their life for my sake will find it.
—Matthew 16:25 (NRSV)

To let go of what I want or what I think I want isn't easy. It is, rather, the patient work of chipping away at the ego's numerous encrusted layers. The only reason someone will put up with whittling away of the self is because she or he has seen a glimpse of the glorious Light. We can't receive this Light when we're distracted and encumbered with "me" and "mine."

The self inhabits a small world that's insecure and fears encroachment. Like the hermit crab, we demand our shell, which protects us from the infinite ocean. To the hermit crab the divine mandate to let go of the shell feels like death. But it is only death to the small world we knew, for a bigger world of primordial freedom. It is death to false self and birth of true self. It is death to "be frantic and pre-occupied with self," and birth to what *Be Still and Listen: Experience the Presence of God in Your Life* is all about.

The infant loses the warm comfortable womb and moves headlong through a canal to a hospital bed, floodlights, firm latex-gloved hands, and uncertainty. It will take years to adjust to that big world beyond the womb, and childhood trust in the goodness of life progresses slowly. But with each step we are encouraged to take another. The tragedy is that somewhere along the line people stop taking steps forward and cling to the security of the shell. Once the hermit crab has taken so many painstaking steps to find just the right shell, do you think it will give the shell up for the unknown? No. The crab will only let go if it's highly motivated by something delectable beyond its shell—something so attractive that the hermit crab will risk everything to behold it.

By some mysterious charm some hermit crabs reach beyond themselves into this unknown. They risk losing everything they have known for something beyond the mind's grasp, which is not found by seeking, yet which only seekers find. The last steps into the mystery of spiritual transformation are characterized by loss, darkness, stumbling, falling. The mystery that is contemplation is never achieved. It is happened upon through dumb luck, otherwise known as grace. The false self is always striving. The true self lets go and lets God.

Die in Order to Become Reborn

Very truly I tell you, unless a kernel of wheat falls to the ground and dies, it remains only a single seed. But if it dies, it produces many seeds.
—John 12:24 (NIV)

The seed knows its own pod—the boundary lines it has always known. This is its comfort zone. To imagine something else is fraught with fear. We fear what we don't know. We fear uncertainty and not getting our way, not being in control. So, the biggest obstacle to transformation is death to what we've known, death to our certainties, to the way it was always done.

Every change is a small death that takes us further along the spiritual path. We become more and more accustomed to letting go and to change. Ongoing transformation, regeneration, and rebirth mark the contours of our true self, always emerging into deeper self-knowledge and love. Eventually the series of changes leads to all-out rebirth, when the seed germinates and moves beyond what it ever imagined for itself. It begins in the Genesis sense of "beginning." This time it does not begin by its own self-promotion, on its own terms, or by its own steam.

When the soul begins in earnest it becomes something entirely different from what it has known. It leaves the little pod—that place of years of comfort and security. It plants roots and moves skyward. It moves from isolated pod to connected tree . . . to connection with the earth, connection with the wrens who perch on its branches, connection with coyote lungs that breathe in its oxygen. Its life is no longer about its small, isolated reality. Its life is now larger—a vast network of interconnection and contribution to a larger whole.

We let go of the small pod so that the big tree can be born. We let go of the safety of the womb and umbilical cord for a new world that waits on the other side. We empty ourselves of what we've known so that God can impart what we don't know. Often when God imparts what we don't know, it will not feel as if we know more. It will feel like darkness. Rebirth and dying are similar.

The infant is scared to leave the comforts of the womb it has always known. It often cries incessantly at the time of birth. It has no idea what is on the outside of mom's tummy. We don't want to leave the comforts of what we have always known. So most of us are petrified of death. At the time of both birth and death we see a tunnel. That tunnel's name is "let go." The more we let go, the less "self" there is. To let go over and over again is abandonment into a higher Self, which we don't and can't understand with our reasoning faculties. We fall into unseen arms. Yet in the end, those intangible arms are the most real, the most substantial, the indestructible core.

Everything related to the senses vanishes. Yet, the Reality that undergirds fleeting phenomena is more substantially "Self" than the passing experiences. This Reality is Experience singular, as opposed to experiences plural. It is the Word singular, as opposed to words plural. So dying to the plethora of words and experiences is really no death at all.

In the same way passing through the birth canal is called birth, not death. To the infant it feels like death. It is death to all the infant has known up to that point. Yet, it is in fact birth. Death of experiences and words in exchange for ultimate experience of the Word is the rebirth of our highest spiritual endowments.

Begin to Participate in Love

If I speak in the tongues of men or of angels, but do not have love, I am only a resounding gong or a clanging cymbal. If I have the gift of prophecy and

can fathom all mysteries and all knowledge, and if I have a faith that can
move mountains, but do not have love, I am nothing.
—1 *Corinthians* 13:1–2 (NIV)

When we forget ourselves and remember God we wake up from the ego's powers of isolation and alienation. We enter the faith of a great family that stretches across generations. In the glow of true self we see all things as they are. We no longer need to separate everything into binaries, into self and others, into conflicting emotions. The true self does not know binaries and conflicting emotions. It knows participation and abiding joy.

The point of centering prayer is "self-forgetting" in the best sense. We become less and less preoccupied with our false self, which is a self-centered construct based on cultural filters. Through centering prayer our motivations become less preoccupied with self. We forget about our own agenda. We begin to ditch many of our plans, and look for ways to support others instead.

The climax of Paul's famous passage on love from 1 Corinthians chapter thirteen is this: "Love is not self-seeking." We become what we seek. So if we seek to satisfy our egocentric self, we will end up puny. If we seek after high art, we will become works of art ourselves.

Most of all, Paul clarifies that compared to participation in love all our trophies are dust. Love is the way to participate most in reality. This may be the most countercultural Christian idea of them all! Love's dynamic sustains all creatures. It's also our very sustenance—our bread from heaven (Exod. 16:4). Without it we crumple.

◼ Questions for Reflection and Discussion

1) "Learn the art of letting go. This is the summary of the spiritual journey." What do you make of this?
2) What do you take away from the story of Jacob wrestling with the angel? Does this story relate to your life? If so, how?

3)   "Love is the way to participate most of all in reality." Do you agree? What might this truth mean for your life?

4)   If you had to guess your "secret name hidden in God," what would it be?

Part Three:

THE UNDIVIDED HEART

Hear O Israel, the LORD your God is one.

—DEUTERONOMY 6:4

I will give them an undivided heart.

—EZEKIEL 11:19

CHAPTER 8

Dominion of God Within

Enter eagerly into the treasure house that is within you. . . .
The ladder that leads to the Kingdom is hidden within your soul.
—*St. Isaac the Syrian*[53]

Kingdom of Heaven is really a metaphor
for a state of consciousness.
—*Cynthia Bourgeault*[54]

Hidden Treasure

A middle-aged woman once said to me in a candid moment: "All I want is to have some really good sex before I die." This sentiment points to the tragedy of our culture.

Even at middle-age some short-lived sensual thrills are considered the end all–be all. This is the bill of goods we are sold through advertising. It is the lie of our sex-and-money culture that keeps us on the surface of life, when all the while there are hidden depths. What we seek is not out there somewhere.

An Orthodox priest recounted this story: A man looked for his elephant. He thought it was nearby. So he searched the perimeter of his house. Then he searched his neighbors' fields. He saw elephant tracks and followed them. Finally, he followed tracks far into the forest. But, still he couldn't find the elephant. So, he gave up the search and headed home. Exhausted, the man arrived home and flung open the front door. There to his utter amazement stood his elephant! He had searched in fields and deep in the forest. And of all places, his elephant stood in his living room. It had been there all along. But, he'd never thought to look there.

This is Jesus's teaching about God—that what we look for out there is really in here. As the Gospel says:

> The dominion of God is like a treasure hidden in a field for years and then accidentally found by a trespasser. The finder is ecstatic—what a find!—and proceeds to sell everything he owns to raise money and buy that field.
> —Matthew 13:44 (MSG)

The biblical hidden treasure is variously called "the kingdom of God, the dominion of heaven, or the dominion of God." The only way to behold it is to sell everything else (Matt. 19:21). Only those who have patiently honed the fine art of letting go are ready for it. Only those who are empty receive it (Phil. 2:7).

When we've found the best, we let go of the good. The good was good when we didn't know about the best. When we know about the best, the good is no longer good. It's a distraction. I'm not implying that my spouse is a distraction. I am saying that my spouse is not my ultimate center of gravity. God is.

If I'm mature in spirit, I will cut the umbilical cords. My spouse, for instance, will no longer be my center of gravity. When we have let go of everything else we can truly be anchored in God's indwelling presence. Then and only then can we have the bandwidth to love our family and friends authentically with less and less self-interest.

Chemical and sexual pleasures, popularity, titles, and impressive hedge-fund portfolios do not compare to the treasure of God's dominion within. The hidden treasure of God's indwelling presence is not subject to corruption and change. It's not tethered to the emotional roller coaster of attachments and aversions. The hidden treasure is categorically different. It echoes freedom through every nook of the soul and through the ages.

Eugene Peterson's *The Message* paraphrase of the Bible says that we find the treasure "accidentally." That's a helpful insight. It's always accidental, and not by our own designs, that we find what's immaculate and everlasting. It's always a sheer gift.

For many, the spiritual journey is another goal-oriented project. It's true: you can knock on the door patiently. Patience holds the key. Yet, the door opens from the other side. The response from the other side is mysterious and totally outside the influence of our agendas. It's never something we "achieve" and is always a surprise.

We're hardwired for self-centeredness. For God to break through our self-serving schemes isn't easy. Only complete transformation can move us from a self-centered life to a God-centered life. It takes an accident, perhaps quite literally a horrifying, life-threatening accident and the subsequent suffering, to crack the self-serving hardpan of the ego. That accidental cracking open leads us to discover the treasure of God's presence and action within.

It's easy to mouth the words, but no small project to undergo transformation. God's map has totally different coordinates, and the old compass is of no use. The topography disorients and is fraught with fear, existential dread, and usually long suffering. And God's timeline is ridiculous. Just ask the Israelites who sojourned in the desert for forty years.

Why would anyone grope in the dark in an unfamiliar land (Gen. 12:1)? Why would anyone endure long years in the wilderness (Num. 32:13)? Because the treasure of God's dominion within is great in its expansive trust and deep fulfillment. It's wise in its unknowing. It's abundant in its connection and participation in a reality much larger than I, me, and mine (John 12:24).

Interior Motivations[55]

[Jesus] continued teaching. "Watch out for the religion scholars. They love to walk around in academic gowns, preening in the radiance of public flattery, basking in prominent positions, sitting at the head table at every church function. And all the time they are exploiting the weak and helpless. The longer their prayers, the worse they get. But they'll pay for it in the end."

Sitting across from the offering box, he was observing how the crowd tossed money in for the collection. Many of the rich were making large contributions. One poor widow came up and put in two small coins—a measly two cents. Jesus called his disciples over and said, "The truth is that this poor widow gave more to the collection than all the others put together. All the others gave what they'll never miss; she gave extravagantly what she couldn't afford—she gave her all."
—Mark 12:38–44 (MSG)

Carl's mother kept a cookie jar atop the refrigerator. And the rule was that one could only eat cookies during meals. Carl's mother said that to sneak cookies in-between meals was a "no-no." She then clarified, "If you sneak a cookie and it's between meals you won't get away with it, because God is watching."

Carl's mother conveyed that God is an external judge. God is in the bleachers watching our every move. If we do well, it's "thumbs up," to use the old symbol from the Roman arena. If we don't do well, it's "thumbs down." This is how many people understand God: God is apart from us and judges our external actions. Pharisees were fixated on following every detail of the law because, like Carl and the cookie jar, God was watching.

What goes with the idea of God as judge is God as distant. Many think God manages the world from a distance. We inherited this worldview from seventeenth-century philosophers—that God is out there somewhere; that God wound up the clockwork of the universe, then stepped back from it all. This is the lie. The truth is that God is organic, not mechanistic. God is a community, not a mechanism.

The idea that God is distant, and a judge of our external actions, is what Thomas Keating and others call the "Western Model of God." People who teach this model imagine that union with God requires climbing an infinite number of stairs. Heaven, where God is, is a remote location somewhere in space. Nobody knows where it is. And access is difficult, if not impossible.

Because we usually consider God as outside of us, we try to please God with external acts, like we would a judge at a gymnastics competition. This model teaches that external appearances are more important than the condition of the heart; that skills or performances are more important than interior motivations. Jesus teaches the opposite.

For Jesus, interior motivations are more important than outward appearances; the dominion of God is within. God looks upon the heart (Matt. 23:26). The two copper coins the widow gave were more significant than the enormous wealth of the elite scribes (Mk. 12:44). Jesus battled the Pharisees on this point. The Pharisees emphasized external acts that placate God and put God on our side. Jesus, on the other hand, emphasized interior motivation and God's dominion within.

Jesus pointed out that the motivation of the Pharisees was respect from peers. They were more concerned about how they were esteemed than about their relationship to God (Matt. 23:24). What's most important to God is not external acts, but internal motivations. The point is not to please God with outward acts of piety but to purify the motivations of our hearts. God could care less about pious displays before our peers. God cares more about the silent prayers we utter when our heart pounds in the night.

Carl thought God hovered over the cookie jar waiting for him to cave to temptation and sneak a gingersnap. A teenager in a video I once saw referred to God as "the one-eyed Cyclops whose eye is always on me." Other teens referred to God as "a policeman." But, Jesus teaches something different. Jesus calls God his "Abba," his "Daddy." Such an intimate reference to God stunned his audience.

Daddy is not a name we use for a distant authority figure. It's the intimate accessible person, who's part of our circle of trust. Later, Jesus adds that "the dominion of God is within you" (Lk. 17:21). In other words, God is not out there somewhere. We're in God and God is in us. We are God's temple (1 Cor. 3:16, 6:19).

Like Carl and the cookie jar, many associate God with fear and punishment, thinking that God is dangerous—a sort of policeman, tyrant, or judge, ready to bring down the gavel and pronounce the verdict: "guilty." This isn't only a caricature; it's a monster we need to erase from our imaginations before it does any more damage.

Keating spoke of a church-sponsored youth retreat. The retreat leaders taught strict abstinence from sex before marriage. Then they showed a video of a teen couple who parked their car at a romantic hotspot overlooking city lights. One thing led to another and abstinence went out the window. Shortly after, on their way home, these teens crashed the car into a tree and died. The attending teens were frightened out of their wits. They got the message loud and clear: God was watching, and if they messed up they would be severely punished. Soon after the video the teens flooded the confession booths. The retreat leaders thought this was a triumph. Yet, this message completely failed to reveal the God of Jesus. The car crash sent a terrible message about God. God is not about fear and punishment. The God of Jesus is about participation, intimacy, trust, and compassion, which leads to service.

A right relationship with God is not fear. Fear may be a mediocre tactic to shake people out of bad habits and get them interested in religion. Yet, mature religion is always based on intimacy with God, trust, and service. Jesus taught that God is even closer than a daddy. For daddy is still a person who lives outside of ourselves. Ultimately no such dualistic image will do.

You Are God's Temple

The dominion of God is within you.
—*Luke 17:21b* (KJV)

You realize, don't you, that you are the temple of God, and God is present in you? No one will get by with vandalizing God's temple, you can be sure of that. God's temple is sacred—and you, remember, are the temple.
—*1 Corinthians 3:16–17* (MSG)

Luke's Gospel states "The dominion of God is within you." 1 Corinthians 3 says this in a different way: "You are God's temple." The Bible affirms that our spiritual faculties, if exercised and developed, can comprehend God who dwells within. Stillness and silence exercise and develop these spiritual faculties. Eventually we will share Jacob's realization at the foot of the heavenly ladder, "The LORD was in this place all the time and I didn't know it" (Gen. 28:16).

Water is of no use unless there's a pitcher to contain it. Then the water can be utilized for life-giving purposes. We are the pitchers. We are vessels of the water that gives everlasting life (John 4:1–42). The early Quakers spoke of "that of God in each person." Thomas Keating refers to "the divine indwelling." Julian of Norwich expressed that we are not only made by God, we are made of God. 1 Corinthians 3 and 6 say we are God's temple.[56] These are different ways to say the same thing.

In *New Seeds of Contemplation*, Thomas Merton wrote that the early prophets and seers of the Bible saw archetypal images of angels, light, and fire. This is how their minds perceived the glory of God. Yet, Merton states that, generally speaking, the grandeur of God is not something we see with our eyes. It's all within us.[57]

It is difficult to get used to this light within. We put a toe in, then a foot, then an ankle. It's so pervasive and brilliant that our eyes squint. Only after an organic process of many years can we open the shutters to let in the everlasting Taborian Light (Matt. 17:1–9, Mk. 9:2–8).[58] The luminous reality of God dwells within, and we gradually learn to adjust our "eyes" to see it.

Participatory Reality

God said to Moses, "I-AM-WHO-I-AM. Tell the People of Israel, 'I-AM
sent me to you.'"
—*Exodus* 3:14 (MSG)

The ultimate reality is "I Am." There's none other. Outside of this
Presence nothing exists. "I Am" is a dynamic unified field of participation
and joy. Everything depends on the great "I Am" for its very substance.
It's the One and only, known to us in a singular Dynamic Unity: "I Am."

God didn't say to Moses "I am a Being." God said, "I am Being
itself"—everything that is participates in "I Am." When we are inside
this flow, all yearning and clutching cease; we are home. We look no
further. And in a flash, we realize that nothing is on the outside of this
flow. Time and space are not external realities imposed by some force
outside of us. Space and time are within us.

An Eastern Orthodox mentor of mine used to say, "I pray God for
you." His omission of "to" was intentional. The point is that God is not
an objective reality outside of us. We participate in the reality we call
God. So, "I pray God" is more accurate than "I pray to God." This is
quantum dynamics. At the quantum level, there's no objective reality.
This is what the mystics call non-dual awareness.

When we measure a thing, we change its nature. For instance, if I
observe a photon of light to be a wave, it will behave as a wave. If I
observe a photon of light to be a particle, it will behave as a particle.
But a photon of light can't be a particle and a wave at the same time.
So when I observe the photon in a certain way, I change the inherent nature of the photon. Photons will conform to our measurements.
Observer and observed are both parts of a singular dynamic. God is a
participatory reality. God is Being on the most essential level: I Am.
And it's impossible to conceive of anything apart from I Am.[59]

Gregory Palamas called "I Am" the "Supraessential Simplicity."[60]
When we awaken to this indwelling singularity everything radiates
like the sun. Then, when I look into my brother's eyes, I look, from a

different angle, into my own eyes. When the underlying unity of all things breaks in on the moment, we're exhilarated.

"I Am" is undifferentiated. This reality, so frightening to the ego, is my lasting security, my true home, my indestructible core. The puny self-centered ego with its insecurities is a passing shadow on this earth. The God-centered "I Am" is the only thing that ever was and ever will be "Real," and which reverberates through the centuries.

Jewish mystics tell us that in our mother's womb we knew God, but at birth we began to forget. The reason we knew God in our mother's womb is that our embryonic selves were awash in the participatory reality of mom. Once we left the womb we began to believe the lie that there is a point at which my skin ends and the universe begins. Nonsense. We are everything we experience. We are part of that eternal flow—I Am. The dominion of God is within us.

Mysticism moves beyond the fleeting, self-centered "I am" to the everlasting, God-centered "I Am." We're constantly tempted to return to the ego's agenda of busyness, manipulation, control, and ambition. Yet, only when we let go and rest in "I Am" do we find our true self, our true Home.

▪ The Questions Determine the Answers

In God we live and move and have our being.
—*Acts 17:28a* (NIV)

I once heard a quantum physicist say, "Electrons behave like school children, eager to give the results the experimenter expects." In other words, what the experimenter looks for is what the experimenter finds.

If we look to creation to reflect God's primordial glory, then that glory will shine through. If our tools are set to measure externally what we already know within, the universe will echo back to us the same sights and sounds that reverberate within. Henry David Thoreau wrote: "The question is not what you look at but what you see."[61] If we experience unity within, we will experience interconnection and unity in our world.

The questions we bring determine the answers. So the questions we bring are primary. The observed phenomena are secondary. With this in mind we learn to set our intentions carefully. We ask our questions thoughtfully, because those intentions and questions contain the answers. It all springs up from within. This explains why people like Saint Paul, who spent so much time in prison, so often radiated joy (Acts 16:25). This explains why Julian of Norwich, whose family was decimated in the Black Plague, so often exuded bliss. If we're preoccupied with outward circumstances, we can't make any sense of these saints.

The interior reality of the saints was completely transformed. It was because of that fire, or should I say that furnace within, that the saints saw light where others saw darkness. Nothing could stop the dynamism and abiding joy of the dominion of God experienced within. Where the world saw an instrument of torture (the cross), Jesus with eyes ablaze, saw the portal to glory.

God is the participatory reality in whom we live and move and have our being no matter if we're in a prison cell, in an anchorite cell, on a mountaintop, or in the shower (see Acts 17:28, Psalm 139:7–13). The furnace of intense belonging and awareness flows from within. Outward circumstances may affect that flow, but they can't stop it.

When this rare idea takes root in us, we are able to deepen a centering prayer practice or some other form of meditation. Wow! To go from a noisy cluttered mind to a quiet mind is a beautiful thing. Then we invoke the Spirit and the Truth, which carries every breath, every thought. We are part of this dynamic eternal flow, not outside of it. The dominion of God is within.

Questions for Reflection and Discussion

1) Were you taught that God is an external reality "out there"?

2) Reflect on the statement, "I pray God for you," omitting the "to" to stress that God is not a reality outside of us. Does this make sense to you? Why or why not?

3) "The questions determine the answers." Is there truth to this? Why or why not?

4) Isaac the Syrian wrote: "The ladder that leads to the Kingdom is hidden within your soul." What do you make of this?

CHAPTER 9

◆ ─────────── ◆

Finding Refuge

*You made our hearts for Thee, O God,
and our hearts are restless until they rest in Thee.*
—St. Augustine

LORD, *my God, I take refuge in you.*
—*Psalm 7:1 (NIV)*

God Is Our Strength

We live in an age of growing interpersonal, national, environmental, and global crises. The presence of these crises in our lives, almost daily, exhausts and dispirits us. These crises repeatedly send the message that our world is insecure and unreliable. Combined with the inevitable personal tragedies of adulthood, the travesties we witness in our communities, in our nation, and in the world can make us want to find a corner in which to curl up and hide.

Over centuries of human history, the anchor that sustained people and communities in the midst of profound upheaval was connection to their Source. To find refuge in God, the First Cause, who knows us better than we know ourselves, is the primary subject of the Bible. Here, I want to tell you some personal stories of how I have found, and been comforted by, God's strength.

◼ River Refuge

*God is our refuge and strength, an ever-present help in trouble. Therefore we
will not fear, though the earth gives way and the mountains fall into the
heart of the sea. . . .*
—Psalm 46:1–2 (NIV)

A beautiful thing about participation in a faith community is expo-
sure to reality as it is. During community prayer times we come to
understand the numerous problems that happen on life's journey, if not
to us, then to the extended church family. When we're part of a faith
community these problems no longer surprise us.

After two decades of pastoral ministry, I've encountered many
human struggles up close. I've visited the bedsides of people toward
the end of life, people with children who've died, people who struggle
with alcohol and heroin dependence. I've visited people who've worked
hard all their lives, but who don't have enough to retire, people whose
parents are terminally ill, who've suffered massive, debilitating strokes.
I've visited people who try to hold down a job and raise their kids, but
to keep up with the bills is a constant stress that chips away their coping
skills. I've visited people in chronic pain after back surgery. They were
told surgery was the cure. And after surgery the chronic pain is worse.
I've visited people whose spouses have died, and people who suffer
from mental illness.

One Sunday afternoon I got a call from the county sheriff. There'd
been a terrible accident and I was needed at the local hospital. A girl
named Cheryl, who was just gifted a brand-new SUV by her daddy for
her sixteenth birthday, sped on back roads with a car full of teens. None
were buckled and the SUV's center of gravity was high. On a sharp turn
at eighty miles per hour, Cheryl lost control. The SUV flipped several
times. The two in the front were thrown from the car's open windows
and arrived at the county hospital dead on arrival. The three in the back
were seriously injured and in intensive care. Cheryl was her daddy's
pride and joy, for whom he would do anything.

Cheryl's dad, Bob, confronted me in a hospital hallway, demanded to see his daughter, and adamantly refused to accept she was dead. I tried to reason with him to no avail. Then finally I called the mortician, who agreed to comply with Bob's demands. In hopes of breaking through Bob's wall of shock and denial, the mortician brought the body of Bob's beloved to the empty high school gymnasium. Bob walked briskly to the mobile hospital bed, lifted the sheet, and demanded that Cheryl wake up. "Wake up, Cheryl, wake up." "Daddy's here." This went on for some time. Then the wailing started. A sound I've never heard before or since, a deep, primal, timeless wailing. Then, both dad and mom slumped onto the lifeless ribcage of their beloved girl and began to heave, shake, and sob.

That night I wondered why I had ever become a pastor. I was beyond the threshold of what I thought I could handle. I couldn't sleep.

Early the next morning by some intuitive grace, I began to walk. I walked until I reached the Yellowstone River. Then I walked the river. There was a wide spot at the river's edge where I sat underneath a huge Douglas fir canopy. I watched the mesmerizing river effortlessly and tirelessly flow. The river soothed my soul. The running water caressed my ears. Tears graced my cheeks. In the years since that day, I have often returned to that green-canopied river refuge.

House of Refuge

As you come to him, the living Stone—rejected by humans but chosen by God and precious to him—you also, like living stones, are being built into a spiritual house to be a holy priesthood.
—*1 Peter 2:4–5* (NIV)

Unless the LORD builds the house, the builders labor in vain.
—*Psalm 127:1* (NIV)

As I've said, my journey of faith started in the mountains. On mountain summits in Yosemite, the King Range, and in Africa the panorama opened and rays of clarity shot through my body. In the thin, crisp mountain air came an ancient knowing. I felt part of something much larger than myself, a web of life that extended from the beginning of time until now. A web of life that intertwined my 3.5 billion-year-old cells with the DNA of mountain ferns.

When life's travails and travesties overwhelm we need a place of refuge. Sacred topographies are powerful examples of this. Wilderness authors Annie Dillard, Mary Oliver, and John Muir wrap me in their fuzzy arms, which resemble high sierra meadows.

A person can be a powerful refuge—someone who has loved us into living, who has showered us with goodness. That person can be a grandmother, a friend, or an arthritic uncle with rivulets around his eyes. These are souls upon whose knobby shoulders we stand, souls who have been softened and deepened by pain. These souls grow tall like Northern California Redwoods with interlocking roots. These souls echo mysterious resilience.

Another source of powerful refuge can be a faith community—a community that has stood the test of years, with a street address, and with leathery hands that welcome you at the door. There is an unspoken assurance that even the broken places are welcome. Communities that genuinely and contagiously care are a healing salve. Community refuges remind us why the original house churches were so potent. The bonds of friendship in such communities give us an unmistakable sense of belonging.

Finally, there are songs or books or pieces of art. For some years, the CD *Chant* by the Benedictine Monks of Santo Domingo de Silos became a refuge for me. When I needed a place to curl and rock, the single tones of the monastery reached out to me through the ages and caressed me. The tongues of sound bathed my sore limbs in an ancient calm. I lay back on my bed with earphones on and within minutes I was home.

In the passage from 1 Peter chapter two, quoted above, the apostle speaks of being built into a spiritual house. I like to think of this spiritual house in terms of the four directions of a compass. The north wall of the house is a place. For me it's an expansive wild place: wildlands. For others, it could be their backyard. When I was growing up my mother loved her rose bushes. I know that our backyard and those painstakingly cultivated roses were Mom's refuge.

The east wall is a person who gave themselves to us freely without self-interest. Such people are rare but they do exist. And when they grace our lives we can't forget it. A series of pictures lines a large window in my office, which looks out over the Sonora Desert. Sometimes I go to the pictures of my beloved teachers and pause at each frame. Occasionally my eyes mist for the graces freely given, which offered direction and hope. The south wall is a beloved community that stands together and carries one another's burdens—a community where friendship and love are recognized by their primary attribute: joy.

When we have been beaten about the shoulders and head with insults, abuses, and carelessness, we need a refuge. We need a retreat—a prayer room, a place in the country, a church, or a home. We need a wild river. A person we can trust through and through. Teachers who shined light upon us and saw gifts in us that we couldn't yet see in ourselves. Or, a book, a musical instrument, an artist, or a favorite movie. Over the years, Scripture has become a refuge for me, especially the Psalms.[62] I read through the New Testament and Psalms every year. Every other day I come across a sentence that gathers me in and opens my windows to the light. All of these sources of refuge have the power to build us up into that spiritual house that 1 Peter promises (see also 1 Peter 5).

Peter also offers the word "cornerstone." Most churches have an original cornerstone with a date etched on it. Yet, the actual cornerstone of our spiritual house is Jesus. More than anything else in our lives, Jesus provides us with his presence in prayer, in the inspiring words of the Gospels, in our houses of worship, in the lives of saints ancient and postmodern, and in our lives of ministry to God and our neighbor. Most profoundly, Jesus offers purely motivated, all-encompassing sacrificial love, which sends ripple effects through the centuries.

Jesus's Spirit rooted and guided our ancestors. It's the refuge that remains when others fall away. Author Nadia Bolz-Weber put it well: "There's this weird thing with Jesus where we touch the eternal."[63] Thank God for the gift of a house of refuge, for each of the four walls, and for the cornerstone that determines the placement of the stones.

The Mountaintop, Part 1

After six days Jesus took Peter, James and John with him and led them up a high mountain, where they were all alone. There he was transfigured before them. His clothes became dazzling white, whiter than anyone in the world could bleach them.
—Mark 9:2–3 (NIV)

One reason why I love to climb is that reaching a new height reveals an altogether different world that stretches the imagination. When I climb, thoughts spontaneously become clear and spacious like mountain vistas. On a mountain, my dreams become vivid.

It's no coincidence that Jesus was transfigured on Mount Tabor (Matt. 17:1–2, Mk. 9:2–3) and that the Ten Commandments were revealed to Moses on Mount Sinai (Exod. 19:20). The prophet goes to the mountaintop, is transformed, and then comes back to transform the tribe. Primal societies such as the Aboriginals of Australia and many Native American tribes vision quest on mountaintops, too. The vision quest, always solitary, and usually accompanied by fasting, is a rite of passage into adulthood and greater responsibility. The mountaintop, it seems, has always been the place of revelation.

The three most famous mountains in the Bible are Mount Sinai, where Moses received the Ten Commandments, Mount Tabor, where Jesus was transfigured, and Mount Zion. We know about the first two, but what about Mount Zion? The Bible repeatedly refers to Zion, which has two primary meanings. First, it is the mountain fortress where David hid from his enemies. So, Mount Zion is a refuge. It is the place where we're safe no matter what assails us. Zion shields us from the catapulting boulders and siegeworks of the enemy.

The second meaning of Zion in the Bible is the place where Solomon built the first temple. The Temple Mount is referred to as Zion. So, Zion is the patch of ground where we build a sanctuary to worship God. It's the place where we lift our voices to Deity. It's the place where we return to sanity—where we come back to our center. May we seek Zion, the mountain refuge. May we seek intimacy and security in the court of the Most High.

But there is a third aspect of Zion I seek, as well. When I climb mountains I encounter fatigue, thirst, rivers to ford, calluses, glaciers to traverse, storms to withstand. These obstacles in turn make me think about the larger obstacles of life—of colossal twenty-first-century problems, such as climate change, terrorism, homelessness, and a billion underfed and undernourished people. When I get to the mountaintop, I still don't understand these things, and yet, something begins to percolate inside of me there: an unmistakable trust. As I gaze out over a high, panoramic vista I begin to see patterns in the apparent chaos—or at least, above the pandemonium, I begin to trust that there *is* a primordial pattern: that there is a God.

On Zion, I trust something deeper than words, as vast as the cloudless sky. May we all seek and find our Mount Zion.

The Mountaintop, Part 2

Six days later, three of them saw that glory. Jesus took Peter and the brothers, James and John, and led them up a high mountain. His appearance changed from the inside out, right before their eyes. Sunlight poured from his face. His clothes were filled with light. Then they realized that Moses and Elijah were also there in deep conversation with him.

Peter broke in, "Master, this is a great moment. What would you think if I built three memorials here on the mountain—one for you, one for Moses, one for Elijah?"

While he was going on like this, babbling, a light-radiant cloud enveloped them, and sounding from deep in the cloud a voice: "This is my Son, marked by my love, focus of my delight. Listen to him."

When the disciples heard it, they fell flat on their faces, scared to death. But Jesus came over and touched them. "Don't be afraid." When they opened their eyes and looked around all they saw was Jesus, only Jesus.
—Matthew 17:1–8 (MSG)

In 2013, I flew from Phoenix to Oakland, California, with my family for my parents' fiftieth wedding anniversary. As I flew I noticed a huge storm was brewing below. There were dark clouds, thunder, turbulence. Yet, the plane soared far above the clouds, where it was absolutely clear. Where I sat, it was totally calm. In that moment I said to myself, "This is the mountaintop experience." This is the experience above the clamor, uproar, and monkey-mind, above the nee nee naa naa. "Nee nee naa naa" is the nature of our minds. When there's a crisis there are flurries of mental activity—flurries of analysis, confusion, speculation—that we can't keep still. Our anxious thoughts jump around like a monkey in a high canopy.

Then I remember that above the clouds it's perfectly calm. When Jesus experienced the mountaintop, he knew the deep calm of all-pervasive acceptance and thorough love that flowed from his Abba. It's easy to get wrapped up in the drama—to get caught up in the turbulence of the monkey-mind. But our higher self is on the mountaintop, in the plane above the tumult, in the upper room (Acts 1:13). Our higher self is above the frenzy.

As the spiritual journey progresses we spend more time on the mountaintop. We discover and rediscover the spiritual faculties of our minds where we're at rest. Where we can let down and trust God. Where we can let go of reason's double-binds and dead ends. Where we can experience peace.

Oh to have a refuge where we don't get caught up in the buzz and swirl! Where we can step back from the dizzying pace. Where we can find sanctuary. The pace of our lives is enough to create turbulence in even the most grounded souls.

Some of the most effective people I know take our crazy world in stride. Not that they don't care. But they care enough to consistently sidestep the drama. When things go beyond a point that they can handle, they have the wherewithal to take a few steps back and give it over to God. Padre Pio, a mystic and healer of our times, said that when situations he encountered were too much, when he was beyond his ability to cope, he would give it over to God. The way Padre Pio put it was to say, "I handle all the things I can. The things that I can't I lay on the cross."[64]

On the road to the cross Jesus didn't allow himself to get caught up in all the drama, anguish, and suffering around him. Part of him was above the fray and in the arms of his Father. Part of him was on the mountaintop above the storm clouds. That's the marvel about mountaintop experiences. They give us unshakable stability that can endure tragedies. As Jesus stumbled under wood beams he remembered the mountaintop. All of us need a place to go above the storm clouds, above the fray.

Jesus experienced all the turmoil of the cross and suffered just as you and I suffer. But surely he had the potent memory of the mountaintop (Matt. 17:5), which buoyed his spirit during his darkest chapters. When we're in touch with our own mountaintop experiences we look up and see the drama unfold around us. We catch glimpses, but then we fall back asleep because we've seen it all before. We're at peace and don't get caught up in the turbulence.

We all have places of deep calm, acceptance, assurance, and refuge to which we can return. My dad walks among his fruit trees. When my mom was alive she lost herself in watercolors, paints, and canvases. Another friend of mine crochets, others fish.

We all need a place to "go," where we can let go of our ordinary plodding mind and experience "the peace of God beyond understanding"

(Phil. 4:7). This place of calm, this abode of trust, this house of rest, is familiar and belongs to us. It's what the writers of *The Philokalia* call our "original nature" or "original purity."[65] This is our true home where we know who we are and whose we are.

Questions for Reflection and Discussion

1) What comes to mind when you think of the word *refuge*?
2) When you hear the phrase "spiritual home" what comes to mind for you? Does your spiritual home have a geographic component or not? Please explain.
3) What does "the mountaintop" look like to you?
4) Is there a place you can go that feels like a refuge? Please explain.

CHAPTER 10

◆ ——————— ◆

Humility and Service

Spirituality . . . is more a journey toward humility
than a struggle for perfection.
—*Ernest Kurtz and Katherine Ketcham*[66]

The true meaning of humility . . . is not self-deprecation or
low self-esteem, but a simple acknowledgment that I am very small,
quickly passing, and insignificant as a separate self.
—*Richard Rohr*[67]

Maximus the Confessor once wrote, "Hold fast . . . to the highest of all blessings, humility, that conserves other blessings and destroys their opposites." The early centuries are full of this kind of teaching. The Desert Elders and the authors of *The Philokalia* valued humility above all else because humility was considered the capstone of Jesus's life among us, and the crown of all the virtues.

As people become more infused with God's presence, genuine humility becomes indispensable. Desert Elders such as Anthony of Egypt and Maximus the Confessor were reported to have extrasensory perception, healing powers, and foreknowledge. Such spiritual gifts exercised without humility and molded around the ego's agenda become disastrous. Yet, when humility is preserved—humility being the essence of a Christ-centered life as opposed to a self-centered life—spiritual gifts will bless one's community.

Disciplined silences in our lives should be ordinary, everyday occurrences. If we've begun to "accomplish" wonderful moments of silence and stillness in our lives, we need to be careful not to congratulate ourselves, for such moments don't originate with us, but with God. These are special times for us—they ought to be that!—but they give no cause for pride.

The depths of the soul are there for every person to discover and explore. The thought of specialness is just one more guise of the ego, which leads to pride. And the Desert Tradition repeatedly warns us against spiritual pride or "self-importance."

According to *The Philokalia*, self-importance is ultimate folly, because it isolates and separates us from one another. Genuine humility, on the other hand, leads to service, and that's the subject of this chapter, because until our contemplative prayer practice begins to transform our lives in the direction of service to others, it remains incomplete.

Imperfection

God said, "The Man has become like one of us, capable of knowing everything, ranging from good to evil. What if he now should reach out and take fruit from the Tree-of-Life and eat, and live forever? Never—this cannot happen!"

God expelled them from the Garden of Eden and sent them to work the ground, the same dirt out of which they'd been made. He threw them out of the garden and stationed angel-cherubim and a revolving sword of fire east of it, guarding the path to the Tree-of-Life.
—Genesis 3:22–23 (MSG)

Therefore, in order to keep me from becoming conceited, I was given a thorn in my flesh, a messenger of Satan, to torment me. Three times I pleaded with the Lord to take it away from me. But he said to me, "My grace is sufficient for you, for my power is made perfect in weakness." Therefore I will boast all the more gladly about my weaknesses, so that Christ's power may rest on me. That is why, for Christ's sake, I delight in weaknesses, in insults, in

hardships, in persecutions, in difficulties. For when I am weak, then I am
strong.
—2 *Corinthians* 12:7–10 (NIV)

Genesis describes an idealized perfect beginning, when Adam and
Eve walked with God in the cool of the evening, where there was no
separation between humans and God (Gen. 3:8). Then there was a
fall from innocence and Adam and Eve were hurled from the Garden.
After Eve and Adam were estranged from the Garden they were rudely
awakened to imperfection.

Most of us long for perfection. We hope against hope to discover
perfect people. When I was a kid, like many children, I thought my
mom could do no wrong. She seemed perfect in every way. When I
first approached the Bible in my late teens I idealized it, thinking it was
perfect. In my early twenties I realized that my parents were flawed (like
all parents). Then when I attended seminary, I realized that the Bible
is divinely inspired, yet passed through many human hands, and as a
result has problems and inconsistencies.[68]

The imperfections of the Genesis patriarchs and matriarchs are
remarkable. Jacob, who is revered as the father of Israel, cheated his
brother out of his birthright (Gen. 27:36). Abraham, who's revered by
all biblical traditions, lied about Sarah. Abraham claimed Sarah was his
sister and not his wife, for fear of the reaction of surrounding tribes if
he told the truth (Gen. 20:2). King David, likewise, who is celebrated
as a person after God's own heart (Acts 13:22), and who had "integrity
of heart" (Ps. 78:72), nevertheless had many personal failures including
adultery and murder (2 Sam. 11).

None of these biblical figures seem to offer models for behavior
today. Perhaps that is why we can understand them. Everyone has dysfunction in their histories and families. Some of us hide it better than
others. But all adults have baggage.

Our tendency to idealize one another and put one another on unre-
alistic pedestals is common. We want to see perfection where it doesn't

exist. Idealization extends to our romantic relationships, as well. Often, when we begin a romance we think our lover can do no wrong, that they're beyond reproach. Later we find out that our spouse has baggage, and exhibits annoying habits, similar to our own.

I once went to a couples retreat with my spouse. The facilitator remarked that two years into a relationship is typically when a couple will experience the icks. Since "the icks" is not a technical term, she clarified. This is when we look at our partner and say to ourselves, "ick, ick, ick." The facilitator said that if a couple can get through the icks they can survive the test of time. The icks is the proverbial hump that we hope to get over. Every person, relationship, community, prophet, job, religion, nation, and epoch casts a shadow.

The immature among us project our shadow outside of ourselves. We point a finger and say, "I see a shadow here and a shadow there." This tendency to point out the shadow externally may have some truth to it. But the deeper truth, as Gandhi said, is to "turn the searchlight inward," to become more aware of our own shadow. This is the mark of humility—what Carl Jung calls "shadow work." The Greek maxim is "know thyself." Jung would say, "know your shadow." Become aware of what you hide, suppress, and deny about yourself, your relationships, your religion, your country.

Shadow work is also the road to the cross. On the road to the cross, we find ourselves, even though we tend to put all the things that challenge and threaten us, including the cross, out of sight. Criminals are put away in prison, the mentally ill are on psychiatric wards, the double amputees are at the veteran's hospital. We like to not have to see what might disturb us—and then we forget that what is disturbing is also found within us. Awareness of imperfection in all its forms is the humble path of redemption.

There was once a student of Zen who went to see a known master and asked for instruction. The master responded, "Tend this garden." So the student tended the garden for a year. Upon the master's return the garden's gate and fence were repaired, the walkway donned fresh flagstones. The garden was raked, weeded, fertilized, and aerated. When the master took a look around, he gave no facial expression and simply said, "You're not yet ready. Work on the garden another year." So, the student doubled his efforts. He arranged the rocks perfectly. He painted the fence and replaced decayed wood. He repaired the tool-shed and organized the tools with racks and labels.

In time the master returned. He inspected the newly organized shed, the immaculate fence, and beautiful rockwork. Then, with a kind smile he responded as before: "You're not yet ready. Work on the garden another year."

Immediately, after the master departed, the student grabbed a nearby rake, then hacked at and scarred a beautiful tree in the garden's center. He hurled and cracked a couple of flagstones. He kicked and skewed fence posts. Finally, he sat in the rock garden and wept.

Over the next few weeks the student let the grass and weeds grow. He let the wind blow errant rocks. Disarray returned to the shed.

A month later the teacher returned. He surveyed the imperfect garden, then sent for the student. This time with deep compassion in his eyes he said in a gentle tone, "Now you're ready."

Vulnerability and Courage

When pride comes, then comes disgrace, but with humility comes wisdom.
—*Proverbs 11:2 (NIV)*

We walk forward in faith. We trust God, who nudges us in the depths of our consciousness. God invites us in dreams and serendipitous moments to glimpse our true life, to get our puny selves out of the way so the real work can begin.

A tragedy of human life is that we often start to realize that maybe there is a "more" and we get interested in religion. Then we have to come to terms with the sham of so much religion. It's tragic if and when we don't allow ourselves to go deeper. We have to manage the vulnerability and courage to sink down into the depths, to feel the pain of the world and to weep, and to find in our faith the resources to be still and silent.

Have the patience to sit on that chair or on that cushion in silent prayer and patiently wait for the mind to become still. As one friend of mine put it, "To sit in silence for even five minutes is brutal." Yet, precisely when we submit to what's difficult, we gain the courage to step from the middle of the herd toward the edge, then finally to wander on our own. That is the grace of monks and hermits.

Be prepared: the contemplative life can bring with it a deep sadness, a sadness that so many people live on the outer rim of the circle of their lives. They don't seem to know that there is a "more." At some point, each person can come to realize that secularism is hollow. It's empty. Sure, there are some beautiful friends who have witty trifles to say that make us laugh. But, under the surface there's hollowness, void of the lasting meaning for which we are hardwired. At some point people also realize that they too often have settled for dull conformity, safety in numbers, and prime-time drivel.

All the while we're hardwired for immensity, intensity, and intimacy! This is life beyond the outer rim of the circle. It's a radiant life that surrenders to God. Life toward the center of the circle humbly lets go and ultimately dies to everything that we hold dear (Matt. 16:25). So we let go of our puny egos that fritter away life posturing, comparing, and contrasting. Toward the center there is a life of unity, harmony, radiance.

Life toward the center requires vulnerability and courage. Henry David Thoreau's words echo through a million pairs of eyes that gaze at glowing screens across suburbia: "The mass of men [women] lead lives of quiet desperation."[69] And what's sad is that many don't even know it. They may even wear a shirt that reads "no bad days." Yet, they are alienated from the God-given dignity that whirls and pulses through their veins. They have replaced the long search for ultimate meaning and truth for a quiet kind of numbness.

The herd will say the radiance spoken of by saints and prophets is bunk, just more naïve nonsense. Then the herd will quote from a religious or spiritual person who purports to express what life is all about, but clearly does not. Meanwhile, people such as Julian of Norwich, George Fox, Thomas Merton, Padre Pio, and numerous other hidden saints shine like the sun. They shine in the midst of their inevitable humanity and dysfunction, which makes them humble and verifies their holiness.

This is the paradox. Saints find themselves in God because they let go of their puny selves. This humility of the saints drops personal agendas and surrenders to the sacrament of the present moment as it unfolds. The self-serving agenda is burned up in the flames of self-emptying (Phil. 2:7). Saints are empty vessels who wait to be filled. It is because of our openness and receptivity to God that God quickens our pulse and bring us abundant life (Ps. 23:3/John 10:10). From that point on our lives are no longer our own. They're an extension of the life of God. And as the saints have witnessed, sometimes a life of abundance and holiness includes civil disobedience and prison time or tragedy. Whatever it is, God, who is closer than our next breath, sustains us.

Sometimes it is helpful to imagine the life of God in terms of God's essence and emanations.[70] God's essence can never be known and will always remain Mystery, yet God's emanations can be known. Like the saints before us, we can become God's emanations—emissaries of the Divine will, full of light and life, no matter the circumstances.

Gentleness

A gentle response turns away wrath, but a harsh word stirs up anger.
—*Proverbs 15:1*

Eventually in any relationship a person can't stop themselves from critique of another. At that point, one's response is everything. When I'm picked on or treated harshly by people I love, which in time is inevitable, I sometimes visualize myself as a garter snake—low to the ground. When I take the low position, I avoid offense.

I wish I were more truly humble by nature, yet my reality and the reality of most people in relationship is that our pride is easily offended. We start to think, *I devoted my life to this person,* or *I sacrificed so much for this family . . . and this is how I'm treated?!* It's then that I visualize the garter snake. I start to think *garter snake, garter snake.* The garden variety creature is authentic and sacred in its ordinariness.

In *The Path of Centering Prayer,* author David Frenette writes that one of the effects of centering prayer in our lives is gentleness. Gentleness is implicit in the third guideline of centering prayer (and you'll find these guidelines, in full, in the Appendix): "When engaged with your thoughts, return ever-so-gently to the sacred word." "Ever-so-gently" is the key, whether in prayer or in life. There's a temptation to get miffed at our errant thoughts and scold them, or at people who disappoint us, and in both cases it almost always backfires. Instead, whenever thoughts arise in centering prayer, we gently return to the sacred word. This gentle approach to our thought processes during prayer nudges us to treat other processes in life and in relationship with tender calm.

My wife was recently agitated because her demanding job makes it difficult for her to achieve a healthy balance between work and the rest of life. So, she was snippy with me. In those moments, I could have easily returned tit-for-tat. I thought of brilliant zingers, and I was tempted to fire back. Then, I realized, *This isn't about me,* and I grew more empathetic of her situation. So, I didn't respond to the snips and started to do the dishes (a clean kitchen makes her feel better).

After a while, when she observed the clean kitchen and that I didn't return snips, she became more serene, and her remarks returned to their usual kind tone. Centering prayer has blessed me. During centering prayer, I've trained my mind to let go of thoughts as they pass through the stream of consciousness. I have also learned—on good days!—to let go of the need to self-justify or exchange tit-for-tat.

Recently, I dreaded weekday mornings. Getting my eight-year-old son up and ready for school was a chore. We would butt heads. I would wake him, then he would get mad and say he was tired. Then I would prod him. Eventually he would start the day reluctantly and grumpily. It was a gridlocked, negative pattern—until one day it dawned on me that I could change the dynamic. Instead of waking him quickly, I set my iPod in his room and turned on his favorite songs at moderate volume. After a few minutes of music, I lay beside him on his bed and talked to him about the day ahead (he likes to know about plans ahead of time). Now, he wakes up happy.

Most people do creative problem-solving in their relationships such as the examples above. In my own life, since my centering prayer practice has deepened, I've noticed that habitual letting go and out-of-the-box ideas come more frequently.

Gentleness with our own thought process helps us exercise gentleness toward others. Centering prayer teaches us to calmly take a couple steps back from our own thoughts. Instead of habitual reactivity, we respond with calmness and compassion. Our responses to people throughout the day become an extension of our prayer practice. As the book of Proverbs reminds, us, a gentle response turns away wrath (Prov. 15:1).

Hospitality

"The Sovereign will reply, 'Truly I tell you, whatever you did for one of the least of these brothers and sisters of mine, you did for me.'"
—*Matthew* 25:40 (NIV)

At a soup kitchen where I volunteer monthly, homeless women and men shuffle past. Some of them clutch the soup bowl and lunch bag that they've been handed, others pause before they wrap fingers around bags and bowls. I notice that many of their fingers are gnarled and stained. Their clothes are often limp and frayed. These fine people have led "tougher" lives, I'm sure, than I have.

The homeless are thick storybooks—volumes that are usually shut to suspicious types like me: pale, laundered, scab-free. But they open sometimes, when they sense trust. At those treasured times, I've heard their stories of abuse, addiction, betrayal, and more than a few Mexican desert border crossings in bloody shoes.

Not much separates me from them. If I'd grown up in a different neighborhood and if my middle-class white privileges had been repealed, the trajectory of my life would've been very different. Middle-class people like me need to stop thinking of our upbringing as normative. It's simply one vantage point among many. These are easy words to write or say, but an entirely different thing to embody. When we stop seeing our histories as normative, walls come down that separate us from one another.

The pony-tailed Native American named Carter, who stands in this homeless lunch line, has a torn ear. The tear took place where an ear-ring once hung. One of life's ambushes assaulted him. Then came more ambushes on Carter. He lost his job. He was evicted from his apart-ment. He didn't have the privileges that I have to fall back on. Carter had no safety net. Instead of moving in with mom and dad or paying for emergency provisions on credit, he was faced with the fact that his dad was in prison and his mom's whereabouts were unknown.

Carter lived out of his pickup for months. Then, a boot was clapped on the back left wheel, before it was towed and repossessed. Now he's on foot. Scraped knees peek through torn jeans. Tomorrow night, while asleep in a park, a junkie will yank Carter's wilted knapsack and run, rifle through it for valuables, then drop it in a dumpster.

I'm no better than Carter. I'm not holier than he. There are hidden saints in this soup line. Jim Wallis, the founder and editor of *Sojourners*, was once in a soup line in Washington, D.C. when a sixty-year-old black woman was asked to pray before the meal. She said, "Jesus, we know you're in this line today. When we meet you help us to treat you right."[71]

The big soup-kitchen pot and ladle I use were donated by my church, a church with Beamers and Cadillacs parked out front. I hold the creative tensions, the in-between places. I dip the ladle into the hearty soup of rice, beans, and chicken, and pour it into another cup. Another worker in the soup line gives a cup to a widow who wears an L.A. Raiders shirt. Immediately her countenance changes. She had been dejected, discarded by the world. "I am a loser" was written on her face. Then she receives that hot cup—tangible evidence that someone in the world actually cares about her. She smiles with ripple effects throughout her face. Of course, solutions to homelessness and hunger are not this simple, yet spontaneous joy in a soup line is a start—a needed spark of hope.

Our own mysticism can never be used to remove us from those who are poor and needy. Instead, it draws us closer, or else it means nothing. The more time we spend in solitude the more compassion percolates. As Thomas Merton, a twentieth-century Trappist monk and author of great books about mysticism, once said: "The Christian mystical tradition is something that has been handed down not only to be talked about but to be *lived*."[72]

■ Downwardly Mobile

So he (Jesus) got up from the supper table, set aside his robe, and put on an apron. Then he poured water into a basin and began to wash the feet of the disciples, drying them with his apron. . . .

After he had finished washing their feet, he took his robe, put it back on, and went back to his place at the table.

Then he said, "Do you understand what I have done to you? You address me as 'Teacher' and 'Master,' and rightly so. That is what I am. So if I, the Master and Teacher, washed your feet, you must now wash each other's feet. I've laid down a pattern for you. What I've done, you do. I'm only pointing out the obvious. A servant is not ranked above his master; an employee doesn't give orders to the employer. If you understand what I'm telling you, act like it—and live a blessed life.

—John 13:3–5, 12–15 (MSG)

The Hebrew verb that means "set aside his robe" is the same one that's used later in John's Gospel to mean, "he laid down his life." So, taking off or laying down his garments is meant to be quite similar to taking off or laying down his life.

Jesus took off his privilege, status, and honors. He took off his robe. He took off the benefits, advantages, and dispensations that came with the titles rabbi, master, messiah, and teacher. He humbled himself (Phil. 2:7). The author of John's Gospel does not see leadership in the same way the world does. In the world, leaders expect to be compensated with bonus checks, the good seats on the plane, and free upgrades.

The foot washing that Jesus does for the disciples was a strange way for the guest of honor to act at his final meal with friends who were also his disciples. What incomprehensible behavior from a ruler who would momentarily announce, "I confer on you a kingdom"! In those days, foot washing was considered so degrading that a master could not require it of a Jewish servant. That's why Peter resisted and basically said, "Master, don't degrade yourself in this way. You shouldn't wrap a towel around your waist and get on your knees. That's beneath you."

But for many Christians, the foot washing stands out as one of the most significant events in Jesus's life. Jesus was known for teaching by example. So, we can't miss the significance. Jesus did this downwardly mobile service before his final day. Thereby, he established the service model. Any who follow Jesus will follow in similar kinds of humble service.

The Jewish and Roman culture of Jesus's time wasn't a whole lot different from our own: the point of life was (and is) to succeed, or get on top, and once on top to stay on top, or else attempt to go further up. Salaries need to be ever-increasing. Houses need to keep getting larger. Vacations, longer. Perks, more of them. But here is a man who was in some ways already on top—who was rabbi, teacher, master to these disciples—who suddenly got down on the bottom and began to wash their feet. In that one act Jesus symbolically overturned the social order. Even his own disciples couldn't comprehend it and were shocked.

Jesus wanted his followers to model downwardly mobile service with their lives. Jesus wanted us to approach the odious smells and the grime in between the toes, to get into the cracks and crevices of broken and dysfunctional human lives. On the evening of the foot washing a dispute arose among the disciples as to who was greatest. Pointedly, Jesus did not deny the human instinct of competition and ambition. He simply redirected it: "The greatest among you should be like the youngest, and the one who rules like the one who serves" (Lk. 22:26). In other words, the dominion of heaven is based on downwardly mobile service.

We hear so often about upward mobility—it is the value of our culture, our country, and most likely, our upbringing. Conversely, the downwardly mobile, who emulate Jesus, get dirty in helping others, become entangled in people's messes, and perhaps even, literally, wash feet (2 Cor. 8:9).[73]

One exquisite example of Jesus's downward mobility is Mother Teresa and the Sisters of Charity. The now-ancient 1986 PBS documentary simply titled *Mother Teresa* is etched in my soul.[74] Why? Because of the pure expression of love found among the Sisters. Throughout the documentary there are images of the downward mobility of the Sisters. The Sisters scrub the wounds of the poorest of the poor on Calcutta's streets, bathe the filth off homeless people with their hands, cut their matted hair, dress their open wounds. When I see those images my eyes mist. Those images speak of a deep love that sets aside agenda, ego, and status, that empties itself in service (Phil. 2:7).

Through Jesus, God accomplished the ultimate downward mobility out of love for us. God put aside throne, crown, royal robes, and tied a towel around his waist. God abandoned privilege, status, and life itself—and as a result, humility and downward mobility are the touchstones today of Jesus's followers. Those who don't embody these don't bear his mark.

▬ Questions for Reflection and Discussion

1) Do you agree that "many people live on the outer rim of the circle of their lives. They don't know there is a 'more'"?

2) "The solution is not to get away from our problems, but to realize that God is totally present and supports us in the midst of them." What do you make of this statement?

3) All relationships, families, communities, religions, and countries cast a shadow, this chapter claims. Do you agree? Why or why not? If so, how pervasive are the shadows?

4) When Jesus washes the disciples' feet he models "downward mobility." What do you make of this? And what do you make of the phrase "downward mobility"?

Cultivate Actual Experience

*Now . . . the personal, mystical, immediate, and intimate is
emerging as the dominant way of engaging the divine.
What was once reserved for a few saints has now become
the quest of millions around the planet—to be able
to touch, feel, and know God for one's self.*
—Diana Butler Bass[75]

If, after reading this book, spiritual freedom born of stillness remains
a mere concept, the book has failed to achieve its purpose. My purpose
is to inspire you to cultivate the actual experience of freedom born of
stillness. Hence the first two words of the book title: *Be Still*.

One of the great contemplative books of the last generation is
Merton's Palace of Nowhere, by author James Finley. (A fortieth anniversary
edition has just been published.) Finley writes, "Prayer never touches us
as long as it remains on the surface of our lives, as long as it is nothing
but one more of the thousands of things that must be done. It is only
when prayer becomes 'the one thing necessary' [Lk. 10:42] that real
prayer begins."[76]

Our underlying communion with God in Christ through silent
prayer and other contemplative arts matters more than the myriad divi-
sions in our hearts and minds. It is the rock that can withstand any and
all storms, and that revives us again and again. It is the exquisite unity
we long for, which puts everything else into perspective. It is what our
divided world needs to hear above the din of the factions and their spin
doctors.

Contemplation is not something we "achieve." We fall into contemplation like falling into a river. Yet, to fall into the river is not enough. We need to learn to swim the river. We need to learn to stabilize the practice of centering prayer. This requires discipline. Any art form worth doing well, such as playing the violin, requires daily practice.

Since the spring of 1999 I have applied the discipline of an athlete to centering prayer, rarely missing my forty minutes of daily centering prayer and my extended yearly retreats. As my own practice became integrated into my busy life as a husband, dad, and minister I explored mystical texts of Christian tradition that spoke to me. I was amazed to find that silence, stillness, and mysticism are implicit in so many passages of Scripture. And I realized that silence and stillness are the starting points of the deepest prayer forms in Christian tradition.

When we have habituated our minds to rest in God, finding God in the center of our being, undistracted and quiet, then we are able to listen like never before. We are able to see. We are able to realize what is true from what is false. We are even able to find creative solutions to what might have previously baffled and confused us. I hope you will share in this journey of daily discipline and spiritual experience. I wish it upon everyone I meet!

Some will dismissively call these mystical forays ways of escaping reality, but they are not that at all. The active, experienced Christian mystic knows that she is entering more deeply and fully into reality than she has ever before. And in that deeper vision of reality, she finds fulfillment and freedom that invigorates her activism. There, in the winter of her spiritual journey she will find the individual and collective dragons that need to be confronted in order for spring to come again.

All relationships grow when given time. Give this one as much time as you possibly can. Our relationship to the deepest aspects of ourselves (see Gen. 1:27)—our relationship with God, will take time. God's love language is "quality time." If we speak that language we will grow in intimacy with the One whom we instinctively long for more than life itself.

We may have to nix other worthwhile pursuits from our schedules, because living consciously and in harmony with self, one another, and the earth depends on it. If you do, I know you will discover that intimacy with God and the consolations of God that follow are the first things. Everything else is secondary.[77] The Desert Elders knew this. We can know it too. The slow plodding of consistently practiced, daily silent prayer, especially in the beginning, is anything but scintillating. Yet, persistent prayer will lead to the everlasting Light!

Questions for Reflection and Discussion

1) This conclusion emphasizes how daily discipline is necessary to discover the benefits of contemplative prayer. Do you think this is true? Why or why not?

2) Do you think it makes practical sense for the contemplation of God to be your top priority? Why or why not?

3) What do you see as your biggest obstacle to a daily centering prayer practice? How might you overcome or "fix" that obstacle so that it no longer stands in your way?

AFTERWORD

A recent survey measures the attention span of the average media-engaged person as eight seconds—a second less than that of a goldfish.[78] It seems our need for constant stimulation and connection has created an insatiable need for something new with almost every breath we take.

But we sometimes mistake our digitized life as one of freedom. After all, we can work from home, order all manner of goods while lounging on a beach, read books without the effort of turning pages, and communicate with friends and strangers without ever speaking a word. We can even join our local congregation online or listen to a quick podcast of a sermon while commuting. There are sixty-second devotionals and five-minute Bible studies.

In this countercultural book, Amos Smith has gently pointed out that for all our connectivity, we are gravely disconnected from our Source. The evidence of our disconnection is seen in many ways. We have an addictive compulsion toward busyness and noise. We tune out instead of probing deeper.

In fact, for all our modern progress, we have lost what the mystics of old deeply understood. We talk about "making time for God" to forge a spiritual connection, when the saints of old experienced God seamlessly in both the extraordinary and the mundane.

Unlike many popular books about spiritual growth, Smith has not offered quick fixes or easy access. There are no lists, no easy exercises, no fill-in-the-blanks. His challenge to us is to embark on a spiritual journey that will take us into a deeply mystical union with God. A union that results in primordial freedom. The call in this book is for a deep, ongoing investment in the practices that lead us toward that freedom.

Smith has diagnosed what undermines many of our public acts of Christianity, including the movements to stand for justice among the marginalized, to protect the environment, and to fight global poverty. Too often we stand on shaky ground, responding to an ego-driven desire to join a movement or appear self-sacrificing. If we don't act out of devotion to Jesus first, we easily burn out, grow frustrated, or become cynical. "Christian" becomes nothing more than an adjective; our work is too important to take time away for reflection or meditation.

As we watch Christian leaders measure success in Twitter followers and Facebook likes, we sense there is something wrong. Accountability in modern Christendom is more often measured financially than devotionally. Even faith-based organization boards rarely ask about a Christian leader's relationship to Christ before they measure the number of contacts with large donors.

When we witness public falls from grace, we are often struck by the audacity of the act that lead such an esteemed leader to crumble. But much like the oak that is toppled by a minor windstorm because the roots have rotted, we often witness a post-mortem confession of a personal spiritual life that has shriveled.

Be Still and Listen is a call to let go of our mindless connections that entangle rather than free us. It is a reminder that to live authentically as Christians we must, at our core, be Christ-followers in a way that defines every breath we take. *Be Still and Listen* has made me think deeply about my own spiritual life and practice. I am confident that this important book has had a similar impact on you.

—Dale Hanson Bourke
Author of *Embracing Your Second Calling: Find Passion and Purpose for the Rest of Your Life* and *The Israeli-Palestinian Conflict: Tough Questions, Direct Answers*

ACKNOWLEDGMENTS

Nothing worth building can be built in a generation.
—*Abraham Joshua Heschel*

I thank all who have believed in my writ and who've encouraged me to write "books," plural. I also thank the Recover Christianity's Mystical Roots (RCMR) network. Rich Lewis and I have worked closely together and have fed off each other in a synergy that is greater than we could have achieved individually.

I give thanks for David Sanford, my cheerleader from the start. He is a selfless networking genius. Many thanks to my copyeditor, Dee Anne Phillips. Her keen eye is a gift! Thanks also to Pam Glenn and Fran Stach, who have spotted numerous grammar, punctuation, and spelling errors.

Thanks to Phileena Heuertz for her eloquent foreword. Phileena is a sister on the path of Mystic Christianity. We have many common teachers and she is one of my guiding lights. Phileena has a gift for making contemplative arts accessible. Phileena, along with her husband, Chris, co-founded *Gravity, a Center for Contemplative Activism* in Omaha, Nebraska. Gravity's publications, videos, workshops, and retreats, along with the personal example of its founders, have aided the transformation of many.

Thanks to Dale Hanson Bourke for her afterword. Dale courageously stands up for justice, which is not about opinion polls and politics. It is about the Gospel of Jesus, which requires us to stand up for immigrants, Palestinians, the homeless. . . . Through Dale, many churches have re-committed themselves to defend the rights of the oppressed (Isa. 1:17).

I give a special thank you to Paraclete Press for publishing *Be Still and Listen* and to Paraclete's publisher, Jon Sweeney. I particularly appreciate Paraclete's emphasis on spirituality, monastic spirituality, and Christian classics.

I give thanks to my family, who has affirmed my daily centering prayer practice, which is the heart of Christian Mysticism for me. When I do centering prayer my eight-year-old son now simply acknowledges, "Dad is in a timeout right now and can't talk." When I seem tense after an intense jag of activity, my daughter says: "Dad, have you done your centering prayer?" My wife graciously allows for my periodic absences and occasionally skirts past my meditation cushion in our bedroom.

I give thanks to my co-workers and to my congregations, who have supported my sustained interest in centering prayer. I also give thanks for the weekly centering prayer groups in the churches I have served.

Finally, I want to thank the congregations I've served as pastor. Your numerous examples of integrity and service have been a light on my path. You have humbled and deepened my spirit.

◆ ──────────── ◆

Centering Prayer Guidelines

These guidelines are provided by Contemplative Outreach, Ltd. I use them in my daily practice, as do tens of thousands of other pray-ers around the world.

1) Choose a sacred word as a symbol of your intention to consent to God's presence and action within.*

2) Sitting comfortably and with eyes closed, settle briefly and silently introduce the sacred word as the symbol of your consent to God's presence and action within.

3) When engaged with your thoughts,** return ever-so-gently to the sacred word.

4) At the end of the prayer period, remain in silence with eyes closed for a couple of minutes.

*A one- or two-syllable word from the Bible is generally best, such as shalom, rest, Jesus, Mary. . . .

**Thoughts include body sensations, feelings, images, and reflections.

NOTES

See the selected bibliography, beginning on page 133, for complete bibliographical information for each title referenced here.

1   This quotation existed in an earlier version of the manuscript that Phileena Heuertz read. It no longer exists in the manuscript's present form. So, in order not to break up the flow of Phileena's Foreword, the quotation was left as written.

2   Keating, Thomas, *Invitation to Love: The Way of Christian Contemplation* (20th *Anniversary Edition*), 109.

3   Kallistos Ware, *The Inner Kingdom*, 89.

4   One of the primary employs of the monks at Qumran was hand-copying Hebrew Scriptures. One of the primary undertakings of the monks in Ireland from Saint Patrick on was hand-copying the Bible (see *How the Irish Saved Civilization* by Thomas Cahill).

5   *Lectio Divina* takes on a number of different forms. The most basic is to select a passage of Scripture for group meditation. After the first reading, the group is asked what word or phrase stands out for them. After the second reading, the group is asked what the verses say to them. After the third reading, the group is asked to offer a prayer based on what the verses are saying to them. Finally, after the fourth reading, the group rests in silence for a designated period. The period of silence can be elongated and can become a designated period of centering prayer.

6   Palmer, et al., *The Philokalia* Vol. 2, 282.

7   See *Mystical Christianity* by John Sanford and *The Gospel of John in Light of Indian Mysticism* by Ravi Ravindra.

8   The Song of Songs is the twenty-second book of the Hebrew Scriptures, found in between Ecclesiastes and Isaiah.

9   Norris, Kathleen, *The Cloister Walk*, 52.

10   I first heard this analogy from a talk by Buddhist author and speaker Jack Kornfield.

11   Kallistos Ware, *The Inner Kingdom*, 93.

12   One of the best studies I've seen on this dynamic is Gus Gordon's book *Solitude and Compassion: The Path to the Heart of the Gospel*.

13   William Johnston, ed., *The Cloud of Unknowing*, 46.

14   Thomas Merton, *New Seeds of Contemplation*, 45.

15   This quotation is the theme for the work of contemplative author Rich Lewis; see www.silenceteaches.com.

16   Kallistos Ware, *The Inner Kingdom*, 79.

17   To foster a deeply rooted centering prayer practice it's important to teach it to children. I plan to do a centering prayer retreat with both of my children when they are ready. A book I would recommend along these lines is *Journey to the Heart: Centering Prayer for Children* by Frank Jelenek.

18   Igumen Chariton, comp., *The Art of Prayer: An Orthodox Anthology*, 43 and 53.

19   We leave behind the senses because the senses deceive us. We see the sun moving across the sky. Scientists confirm that this is an illusion. The sun is stationary and the earth is moving. We see water in the desert. We arrive at the water and it disappears. It was a mirage. In other words, our senses deceive us. The mystics take this understanding a step further. . . . What is ultimately real cannot be apprehended by the senses. What is ultimately real is apprehended by what the writers of *The Philokalia* refer to as our "spiritual faculties."

20   John Cassian, *The Conferences*, conference with Abba Moses.

21   Kallistos Ware, *The Orthodox Way*, 47–49.

22   *The Book of the Poor in Spirit by a Friend of God* illuminates the possibility of being "lifted above the senses into pure silence" (151). This pure silence is not just about the mind. It's about the healing of the entire nervous system and the deep peace which follows. It is a holistic peace and the whole is greater than the sum of the parts.

23   Thomas Merton, *New Seeds of Contemplation*, 234.

24   There is danger in the path of daily discipline, because spiritual consolations can be seen as a goal to "achieve" like other athletic goals. This is dangerous because we can start to think we arrive at spiritual consolations as a result of our own discipline and effort. This leads to pride, which is spiritual destruction according to the Desert Tradition.

25   Gregory most likely got the phrase "Rest in God" from Psalm 62:5.

26   Pope Francis; see https://www.ncronline.org/blogs/francis-chronicles/popes -quotes-mystics.

27   Matthew Fox, *Meister Eckhart: A Mystic-Warrior for Our Times*, 146. Fox is describing the ideas of French philosopher Gaston Bachelard.

28   Some exemplars of nature mysticism in Christian tradition are Francis of Assisi, St. Patrick, Celtic spirituality, John Muir, and Annie Dillard.

29   John Muir, *John of the Mountains: The Unpublished Journals of John Muir*, 92.

30   Fred Hoyle, *The Mathematics of Evolution*.

31   Annie Dillard, *Holy the Firm*.

32   James Finley, *Merton's Palace of Nowhere*, 17.

33   J. Rufus Fears shares this point of view in *Books That Have Made History: Books That Can Change Your Life*, CD 2, lecture 6 on the Gospel of Mark.

34   Thomas Merton, *New Seeds of Contemplation*, 54.

35   Richard Foster, *Celebration of Discipline*, "The Discipline of Solitude" chapter.

36   John Climacus, *The Ladder of Divine Ascent*, 1.

37   Palmer, et al., *The Philokalia* Vol. 1, 176.

38   Palmer, et al., *The Philokalia* Vol. 2, 73.

39   Palmer, et al., *The Philokalia* Vol. 3, 314.

40   I like these healing words of Thomas Keating: "Most often 'original sin' does not pertain to anything you have done. It pertains to what was done to you, especially childhood."

41   Palmer, et al., *The Philokalia* Vol. 3, 314.

42   Barbara Brown Taylor, *The Luminous Web*, chapter 4.

43   The Greeks referred to the divine *Logos*. The *Logos* is the pre-existent Word, which became incarnate in Jesus in the fullness of time.

44   This story is my retelling of a story Thomas Keating tells in his book *Intimacy with God: An Introduction to Centering Prayer.*

45   Paulo Coelho, *The Alchemist*, 90.

46   Elbert Hubbard, *Elbert Hubbard: A Treasury of Insights, Inspiration, and Provocations*, 98.

47   www.pbs.org/wnet/african-americans-many-rivers-to-cross/history/how-many-slaves-landed-in-the-us/.

48   Some might claim that they are superior in strength and that "weakness" is not in their vocabulary. I have met such chiseled and armed characters. Yet I would say that their weakness is that they're not in touch with their heart. Because the heart is inherently soft and weak. And to be human is to feel empathy for our fellow humans. Empathy makes us vulnerable. It also makes us truly human and truly beautiful after the manner of Christ.

49   Thomas Keating, *Open Mind, Open Heart*, definition of "Transformation" in glossary, 147.

50   These two commandments have their basis in Hebrew Scripture: Deuteronomy 6:4, Leviticus 19:18.

51   Thomas Merton, *New Seeds of Contemplation*, 33.

52   Gregory Boyle, *Tattoos on the Heart*, 53–54.

53   St. Isaac the Syrian, *The Ascetical Homilies of St. Isaac the Syrian*, 11.

54   Cynthia Bourgeault, *The Wisdom Jesus*, 30.

55   This section is inspired by talks given by Thomas Keating. Sometimes in this chapter I follow Keating's storyline almost verbatim.

56   1 Corinthians 3:16, 6:19.

57   Thomas Merton, *New Seeds of Contemplation*, 41–42.

58   It is telling that both George Fox and the early Quakers and the Orthodox emphasize the Christ Light.

59   Paul Tillich's phrase "The Ground of All Being" is a contemporary translation of "I Am who I Am."

60   Palmer, et al., *The Philokalia* Vol. 4, 423.

61   Henry David Thoreau, *I to Myself: An Annotated Selection from the Journal of Henry David Thoreau*, 86.

62   The Psalms offend a lot of people. The violent tribal times in which they were written is daunting. For those who find the Psalms challenging, I might recommend *Psalms for Praying* by Nan Merrill. Merrill's fresh translation draws out the prayerful essence of the Psalms.

63   Nadia Bolz-Weber, "Frustrated & Saved by Jesus" video, http://www. theworkofthepeople.com/frustrated-and-saved-by-jesus.

64   Sergio Castellitto (actor) and Carlo Carlei (director), *Padre Pio Miracle Man* DVD.

65   Palmer, et al., *The Philokalia* Vol. 3, 314.

66   Ernest Kurtz and Katherine Ketcham, *The Spirituality of Imperfection*, 5.

67   Richard Rohr, "Mystics and Non-Dual Thinkers: Week 3: John of the Cross, Part 3: Humility," July 31, 2015. See http://cac.org/john-cross-part-iii-humility-2015-07-31/.

68   One brief example of Scriptures' inconsistencies is the story of David and Goliath. There are three vastly different renditions of the story in Scripture.

69   Henry David Thoreau, *Walden*, Chapter 1A.

70   This is a distinction first articulated by Gregory Palamas.

71   Jim Wallis, https://sojo.net/articles/lord-help-us-treat-you-well.

72   Thomas Merton, *A Course in Christian Mysticism*, xix.

73   To my knowledge, Henri Nouwen was the first to write about "downward mobility." He used this term to describe the life of Jesus. He then embodied it in his own life when he left his job as a professor at Harvard University to take care of a severely disabled man named Adam at L'Arche Community in Canada.

74   http://www.amazon.com/Mother-Teresa-Narration-Richard-Attenborough/dp/B000WOYRUI.

75   Diana Butler Bass, *Grounded: Finding God in the World—A Spiritual Revolution*, 26.

76   James Finley, *Merton's Palace of Nowhere*, 17.

77   Matthew 6:33.

78   Microsoft survey reported in *Time*, May 14, 2015, available online at http://time.com/3858309/attention-spans-goldfish/.

SELECTED BIBLIOGRAPHY

I have found the following books to be life-giving. I recommend that you peruse them and see if there are familiar authors or particular themes that catch your eye, then add them to your reading list. I don't know about you, but I am a lover of audio books and always listen to books on my daily commute. Your local library can be an excellent source for audio versions of these books. May you find a handful of titles in whatever form and may they invigorate you and spark your imagination.

Aslan, Reza. *Beyond Fundamentalism*. New York: Random House, 2010.

Bailey, Kenneth. *Poet and Peasant*. Grand Rapids, MI: Eerdmans, 1976.

————. *Jesus through Middle-Eastern Eyes*. Westmont, IL: IVP Academic, 2011.

Bass, Diana Butler. *Grounded: Finding God in the World—A Spiritual Revolution*. San Francisco: HarperOne, 2015.

Bauckham, Richard. *Jesus and the Eyewitnesses*. Grand Rapids, MI: Eerdmans, 2006.

Beals, Timothy J. *The Red Letters: The Sayings and Teachings of Jesus*. Wheaton, IL: Crossway, 2009.

Benedictine Monks of Santo Domingo of Silo. *Chant*. Audio CD.

Berry, Wendell. *The Unsettling of America: Culture & Agriculture*. Berkeley, CA: Counterpoint, 1996.

Blumhardt, Christoph Friedrich. *Everyone Belongs to God: Discovering the Hidden Christ*. Walden, PA: Plough, 2015.

The Book of the Poor in Spirit by a Friend of God (A Guide to Rhineland Mysticism), edited and trans. by C. F. Kelly. New York: Longmans, Green, & Co., 1955.

Bourgeault, Cynthia. *Centering Prayer and Inner Awakening*. Cambridge, MA: Cowley, 2004.

————. *The Meaning of Mary Magdalene: Discovering the Woman at the Heart of Christianity*. Boston, MA: Shambhala, 2010.

————. *The Wisdom Jesus: Transforming Heart and Mind—A New Persceptive on Christ and His Message*. Boston, MA: Shambhala, 2008.

Bourke, Dale Hanson, *Embracing Your Second Calling: Find Passion and Purpose for the Rest of Your Life*. Nashville, TN: Thomas Nelson, 2010.

Boyle, Gregory. *Tattoos on the Heart: The Power of Boundless Compassion*. New York: Free Press, 2010.

Brinton, Howard. *Friends for 300 Years*. Wallingford, PA: Pendle Hill Publications, 1993.

Brock, Rita Nakashima, and Gabriella Lettini. *Soul Repair: Recovering from Moral Injury after War*. Boston: Beacon Press, 2013.

Buddhaghosa, Bhadantacariya. *The Path of Purification: Visuddhimagga*, trans. Bhikkhu Nanamoli. Onalaska: Pariyatti Publishing, 2003.

Cahill, Thomas. *The Gift of the Jews: How a Tribe of Desert Nomads Changed the Way Everyone Thinks and Feels*. New York: Anchor Books, 2010.

———. *How the Irish Saved Civilization: The Untold Story of Ireland's Heroic Role from the Fall of Rome to the Rise of Medieval Europe*. New York: Anchor Books, 1996.

Cassian, John. *The Conferences*. Amazon Digital Services, Inc., 2010.

Chariton, Igumen, comp. *The Art of Prayer: An Orthodox Anthology*. London: Faber & Faber, 1997.

Chittister, Joan. *Between the Dark and the Daylight: Embracing the Contradictions of Life*. New York: Image, 2015.

Chitty, Derwas James. *The Desert a City: An Introduction to the Study of Egyptian and Palestinian Monasticism Under the Christian Empire*. New York: Saint Vladimir's Seminary Press, 1977.

Christensen, Michael J., and Jeffrey A. Wittung, eds. *Partakers of the Divine Nature: The History and Development of Deification in the Christian Traditions*. Grand Rapids, MI: Baker Academic, 2007.

Christie, Douglas. *The Blue Sapphire of the Mind: Notes for a Contemplative Ecology*. New York: Oxford University Press, 2012.

Chryssavgis, John. *In the Heart of the Desert: The Spirituality of the Desert Fathers and Mothers*. Bloomington, IN: World Wisdom, 2008.

Chumley, Norris. *Mysteries of the Jesus Prayer: Experiencing the Presence of God and a Pilgrimage to the Heart of an Ancient Spirituality*. New York: HarperOne, 2011.

Claiborne, Shane. *The Irresistible Revolution: Living as an Ordinary Radical*. Grand Rapids, MI: Zondervan, 2006.

Climacus, John. *The Ladder of Divine Ascent* (Classics of Western Spirituality). Mahwah, NJ: Paulist Press, 1988.

The Cloud of Unknowing and the Book of Privy Counseling, edited by William Johnston. NewYork: Image, 1996.

Coelho, Paulo. *The Alchemist*. New York: HarperOne, 1988.

Coffin, William Sloan. *The Heart Is a Little to the Left: Essays on Public Morality*. Lebanon, NH: University Press of New England, 2011.

Cyril of Alexandria. *The Unity of Christ*. Yonkers, NY: Saint Vladimir's Seminary Press, 2000.

De Caussade, Jean-Pierre. *Abandonment to Divine Providence*. Mineola, NY: Dover, 2008.

———. *The Sacrament of the Present Moment*. New York: HarperSanFrancisco, 2009.

Dillard, Annie. *Holy the Firm*. New York: Perennial, 1988.

Dionysius the Areopagite. *The Divine Names and the Mystical Theology*, trans. by C.E. Rolt. Mineola, NY: Dover, 1994.

Dorhauer, John. *Beyond Resistance: The Institutional Church Meets the Postmodern World.* Chicago: Exploration Press, 2015.

Epperly, Bruce G. *Process Theology: Embracing Adventure with God.* Gonzalez, FL: Energion Publications, 2011.

Fears, J, Rufus. *Books That Have Made History: Books That Can Change Your Life.* Chantilly, VA: The Teaching Company, 2005.

Finley, James. *Christian Meditation: Experiencing the Presence of God.* New York: Harper One, 2005.

———. *Merton's Palace of Nowhere.* Notre Dame, IN: Ave Maria Press, 2003.

Foster, Richard J. *Celebration of Discipline: The Path to Spiritual Growth.* New York: HarperSanFrancisco, 2002. Especially chapters 2, 4, 6, and 7.

Fox, George. *The Journal of George Fox.* Barnesville, OH: Friends United Press, 2006.

Fox, Matthew. *Meister Eckhart: A Mystic-Warrior for Our Times.* Novato, CA: New World Library, 2014.

Frenette, David. *The Path of Centering Prayer: Deepening Your Experience of God.* Louisville, CO: Sounds True, 2012.

Gold, Victor Roland, et al. *The New Testament and Psalms: An Inclusive Version.* New York: Oxford University Press, 1995.

Gordon, Gus. *Solitude and Compassion: The Path to the Heart of the Gospel.* Maryknoll, NY: Orbis, 2014.

Gore, Al. *An Inconvenient Truth: The Planetary Emergency of Global Warming and What We Can Do about It.* New York: Rodale Books, 2006.

———. *An Inconvenient Sequel: Truth to Power.* Documentary Film, 2017.

Gorg, Peter. *The Desert Fathers: Saint Anthony and the Beginning of Monasticism.* San Francisco: Ignatius Press, 2011.

St. Gregory Palamas. *Holy Hesychia: The Stillness That Knows God.* Bucharest, Romania: Pleroma, 2016.

Hedges, Chris. *War Is a Force That Gives Us Meaning.* New York: Public Affairs, 2014.

Heuertz, Phileena. *Journey of a Soul: Contemplative Spirituality for the Active Life.* Downers Grove, IL: InterVarsity Press, 2010.

Holman, Kimberly. *Pray without Ceasing: The Transformative Power of a Prayerful Attitude.* Kimberly Holman, 2014.

Hoyle, Fred. *The Mathematics of Evolution.* Wauconda, IL: Acorn Enterprises, 1999.

Hua Ching, Ni. *The Complete Works of Lao Tzu: Tao Teh Ching and Hau Hu Ching.* Santa Monica, CA: Sevenstar Communications, 1995.

Hubbard, Elbert. *A Message to Garcia: And Other Essential Writings on Success.* Best Success Books, 2014.

———. *Elbert Hubbard: A Treasury of Insights, Inspiration, and Provocations,* ed. Sam Torode. CreateSpace Independent Publishing, 2016.

St. Isaac the Syrian. *The Ascetical Homilies of St. Isaac the Syrian.* Brookline, MA: Holy Transfiguration Monastery, 2011.

Jelenek, Frank. *Journey to the Heart: Centering Prayer for Children*. Brewster, MA: Paraclete Press, 2007.

John of the Cross. *The Collected Works of St. John of the Cross*. Washington, DC: Institute for Carmelite Studies, 1991.

Johnston, William. *Christian Zen: A Way of Meditation*. Bronx: Fordham University Press, 1997.

Jones, Ann. *They Were Soldiers: How the Wounded Return from America's Wars*. Chicago: Haymarket Press, 2014.

Jones, Rufus M. *The Faith and Practice of the Quakers*. Whitefish, MT: Kessinger, 2008.

Jung, C. G. *The Undiscovered Self*. New York: Mentor Books, 1958.

Keating, Thomas. *Contemplative Prayer: Traditional Christian Meditations for Opening to Divine Union*. Louisville, CO: Sounds True Audio, 2004.

———. *Intimacy with God: An Introduction to Centering Prayer*. New York: Crossroad, 2009.

———. *Invitation to Love: The Way of Christian Contemplation* (20th Anniversary Edition). New York: Continuum, 2013.

———. "Method of Centering Prayer," online at http://www.contemplativemind. org/practices/subnav/prayer.htm.

———. *Open Mind, Open Heart: The Contemplative Dimension of the Gospel*. New York: Continuum, 1995.

Kurtz, Ernest, and Katherine Ketcham. *The Spirituality of Imperfection: Storytelling and the Search for Meaning*. New York: Bantam, 2008.

Lossky, Vladimir. *The Mystical Theology of the Eastern Church*. Crestwood, NY: St. Vladimir's Seminary Press, 2002.

Marshall, George. *Don't Even Think About It: Why Our Brains Are Wired to Ignore Climate Change*. New York: Bloomsbury, 2014.

McDonnell, Thomas P., ed. *A Thomas Merton Reader*. Garden City, NY: Image Books, 1974.

McGinn, Bernard, and Patricia Ferris. *Early Christian Mystics: The Divine Vision of Spiritual Masters*. New York: Crossroad, 2003.

McGinn, Bernard, ed. *The Essential Writings of Christian Mysticism*. New York: Modern Library, 2006.

McIntosh, Kenneth. *Water from an Ancient Well: Celtic Spirituality for Modern Life*. Vestal, NY: Anamchara Books, 2011.

McKibben, Bill. *Maybe One: A Case for Smaller Families*. New York: Plume, 1999.

Meinardus, Otto F. A. *Coptic Saints and Pilgrimages*. Cairo: American University in Cairo Press, 2004.

Meninger, William A. *The Loving Search for God: Contemplative Prayer and the Cloud of Unknowing*. New York: Continuum, 1998.

Merrill, Nan C. *Psalms for Praying: An Invitation to Wholeness*. New York: Continuum, 2007.

Merton, Thomas. *A Course in Christian Mysticism*, ed. Jon M. Sweeney. Collegeville, MN: Liturgical Press, 2017.

———.*Gandhi on Nonviolence*. New York: New Directions, 2007.

———. *New Seeds of Contemplation*. New York: New Directions, 1972.

———. *The Way of Chuang Tzu*. New York: New Directions, 2010.

———. *The Wisdom of the Desert*. New York: New Directions, 1970.

Metz, Johann. *Faith in History and Society: Toward a Practical Fundamental Theology*. New York: Crossroad Publishing, 2007.

Miles, Jack. *God: A Biography*. New York: Vintage Books, 1996.

Muir, John. *John of the Mountains: The Unpublished Journals of John Muir*, ed. Linnie Marsh. Wolfe Madison, WI: University of Wisconsin Press, 1979.

Mulholland Jr., M. Robert. *Shaped by the Word: The Power of Scripture in Spiritual Formation*. Nashville: Upper Room, 2001.

Nolan, Albert. *Jesus Today: A Spirituality of Radical Freedom*. Maryknoll, NY: Orbis Books, 2006.

Norris, Kathleen. *Amazing Grace: A Vocabulary of Faith*. New York: Riverhead Books, 1999.

———. *The Cloister Walk*. New York: Riverhead Books, 1996.

———. *The Psalms*. New York: Riverhead Books, 1997.

Nouwen, Henri J. M. *The Living Reminder: Service and Prayer in Memory of Jesus Christ*. New York: HarperOne, 2009.

——— *The Wounded Healer: Ministry in Contemporary Society*. New York: Image Books, 1979.

Oliver, Mary. *Upstream: Selected Essays*. New York: Penguin Press, 2016.

Palmer, Parker J. *A Hidden Wholeness: The Journey toward an Undivided Life*. San Francisco: Jossey-Bass, 2004.

———. *The Promise of Paradox: A Celebration of Contradictions in the Christian Life*. San Francisco: Jossey-Bass, 2008.

Palmer, G.E.H., et al. *The Philokalia: The Complete Text Vol. 1–4*, compiled by St. Nikodimos of the Holy Mountain and St. Makarios of Corinth. London: Faber and Faber, 1983–95. I suggest starting with volume 2, which focuses on Maximus the Confessor.

Panikkar, Raimon. *The Cosmotheandric Experience: Emerging Religious Consciousness*. Maryknoll, NY: Orbis Books, 1993.

Pennington, M. Basil. *Centering Prayer: Renewing an Ancient Christian Prayer Form*. Garden City, NY: Doubleday, 1980.

Peterson, Eugene H. *The Message Remix: The Bible in Contemporary Language*. Colorado Springs: NavPress, 2012.

Ponticus, Evagrius. *The Praktikos and Chapters on Prayer*. Kalamazoo, MI: Cistercian Publications, 1981.

Public Broadcasting Service (PBS) documentary. *Mother Teresa.* Aired November 28, 1986. Ann and Jeanette Petrie, directors.

Ravindra, Ravi. *The Gospel of John in Light of Indian Mysticism.* Rochester, VT: Inner Traditions, 2004.

Remarque, Erich Maria. *All Quiet on the Western Front.* New York: Ballantine Books, 1987.

Rensberger, David. "The Desert." *Weavings* magazine (XVI/3), May/June 2001.

Robinson, Anthony. *What's Theology Got to Do with It? Convictions, Vitality, and the Church.* Herndon, VA: The Alban Institute, 2006.

Rohr, Richard. *The Art of Letting Go: Living the Wisdom of Saint Francis.* Louisville, CO: Sounds True, 2010.

———. *Everything Belongs: The Gift of Contemplative Prayer.* New York: Crossroad, 2003.

———. *Falling Upward: A Spirituality for the Two Halves of Life.* San Francisco: Jossey-Bass, 2011.

———. *The Immortal Diamond: Searching for Our True Self.* San Francisco: Jossey-Bass, 2013.

———. *The Naked Now: Learning to See as the Mystics See.* New York: Crossroad, 2009.

———. *What the Mystics Know: Seven Pathways to Your Deeper Self.* New York: Crossroad Publishing, 2015.

Sample, Tex. *Earthy Mysticism.* Nashville: Abingdon Press, 2008.

Samuel, V.C. *The Council of Chalcedon Re-Examined.* London: British Orthodox Press, 2001.

Sanford, David. *If God Disappeared: 9 Faith Wreckers and What to Do about Them.* Goodyear, AZ: Salt River Press, 2008.

Sanford, John A. *Mystical Christianity: A Psychological Commentary on the Gospel of John.* New York: Crossroad, 1997.

Schmemann, Alexander. *For the Life of the World: Sacraments and Orthodoxy.* New York: Saint Vladimir's Press, 1997.

Sendak, Maurice. *Where the Wild Things Are.* New York: HarperCollins, 1984.

Sinetar, Marsha. *Ordinary People as Monks and Mystics.* Mahwah, NJ: Paulist Press, 2007.

Smith, Amos. *Healing the Divide: Recovering Christianity's Mystic Roots.* Eugene, OR: Wipf & Stock, 2013.

Smith, Huston. *Forgotten Truth: The Common Vision of the World's Religions.* New York: HarperOne, 1997.

———. *The Soul of Christianity: Restoring the Great Tradition.* New York: HarperOne, 2005.

Stace, Walter T., ed. *The Teachings of the Mystics: Selections from the Great Mystics and Mystical Writings of the World.* New York: The New American Library, 1960.

Strobel, Lee. *The Case for a Creator: A Journalist Investigates Evidence That Points toward God.* Grand Rapids, MI: Zondervan, 2004.

Strunk, William, and E.B. White. *The Elements of Style.* New York: Pearson, 1999.

Talbot, John Michael. *The Universal Monk: The Way of the New Monastics*. Collegeville, MN: Liturgical Press, 2011.

Taylor, Barbara Brown. *Learning to Walk in the Dark*. New York: Harper One, 2015.

———. *The Luminous Web: Essays on Science and Religion*. Cambridge, MA: Cowley Publications, 2000.

Teresa of Avila. *Interior Castle*. Mineola, NY: Dover Publications, 2007.

Thaddeus of Vitovnica. *Our Thoughts Determine Our Lives*. Platina, CA: St. Herman of Alaska Brotherhood, 2009.

Thiede, Carsten Peter, and Matthew d'Ancona. *Eyewitness to Jesus: Amazing New Manuscript Evidence about the Origin of the Gospels*. New York: Doubleday, 1996.

Thoreau, Henry David. *I to Myself: An Annotated Selection from the Journal of Henry David Thoreau*, ed. Jeffery S. Cramer. New Haven: Yale University Press, 2007.

———. *Walden*. Various editions.

Tickle, Phyllis. *The Great Emergence: How Christianity Is Changing and Why*. Grand Rapids, MI: Baker Books, 2008.

Tolstoy, Leo. *The Law of Love and the Law of Violence*. Mineola, NY: Dover, 2010.

Underhill, Evelyn. *Mysticism: A Study in the Nature and Development of Spiritual Consciousness*. Mineola, NY: Dover, 2002.

Walsh, Roger, and Frances Vaughan. *Paths beyond Ego: The Transpersonal Vision*. New York: Tarcher, 1993.

Ware, Kallistos. *The Inner Kingdom, Volume 1 of the Collected Works*. New York: St. Vladimir's Seminary Press, 2000.

———. *The Orthodox Way*. New York: St. Vladimir's Seminary Press, 1995.

Whitehead, Alfred North. *Process and Reality (Gifford Lectures Delivered in the University of Edinburgh During the Session 1927-28)*. New York: Free Press, 1979.

Whitman, Walt. *Leaves of Grass: The Original 1855 Edition*. Mineola, NY: Dover, 2007.

Wilber, Ken. *The Integral Vision: A Very Short Introduction to the Revolutionary Integral Approach to Life, God, the Universe, and Everything*. Boston: Shambhala, 2007.

———. *No Boundary: Eastern and Western Approaches to Spiritual Growth*. Boston: Shambhala, 2001.

Wilson-Hartgrove, Jonathan. *New Monasticism: What It Has to Say to Today's Church*. Grand Rapids, MI: Brazos, 2008.

Wink, Walter. *Engaging the Powers: Discernment and Resistance in a World of Domination*. Minneapolis: Augsburg Fortress, 1992.

———. *Jesus and Nonviolence: A Third Way*. Minneapolis: Fortress Press, 2003.

———. *The Powers That Be: Theology for a New Millennium*. New York: Three Rivers Press, 1999.

Zinn, Howard. *A People's History of the United States*. New York: Harper Perennial, 2005.

ABOUT PARACLETE PRESS

Who We Are

As the publishing arm of the Community of Jesus, Paraclete Press presents a full expression of Christian belief and practice—from Catholic to Evangelical, from Protestant to Orthodox, reflecting the ecumenical charism of the Community and its dedication to sacred music, the fine arts, and the written word. We publish books, recordings, sheet music, and DVDs that nourish the vibrant life of the church and its people.

What We Are Doing

Books

Paraclete Press books show the richness and depth of what it means to be Christian. While Benedictine spirituality is at the heart of who we are and all that we do, our books reflect the Christian experience across many cultures, time periods, and houses of worship.

We have many series, including *Paraclete Essentials; Paraclete Fiction; Paraclete Giants;* and the new *The Essentials of...,* devoted to Christian classics. Others include *Voices from the Monastery* (men and women monastics writing about living a spiritual life today), *Active Prayer,* the award-winning *Paraclete Poetry,* and new for young readers: *The Pope's Cat.* We also specialize in gift books for children on the occasions of Baptism and First Communion, as well as other important times in a child's life, and books that bring creativity and liveliness to any adult spiritual life.

The Mount Tabor Books series focuses on the arts and literature as well as liturgical worship and spirituality; it was created in conjunction with the Mount Tabor Ecumenical Centre for Art and Spirituality in Barga, Italy.

Music

The Paraclete Recordings label represents the internationally acclaimed choir *Gloriæ Dei Cantores,* the *Gloriæ Dei Cantores Schola,* and the other instrumental artists of the *Arts Empowering Life Foundation.*

Paraclete Press is the exclusive North American distributor for the Gregorian chant recordings from St. Peter's Abbey in Solesmes, France. Paraclete also carries all of the Solesmes chant publications for Mass and the Divine Office, as well as their academic research publications.

In addition, Paraclete Press Sheet Music publishes the work of today's finest composers of sacred choral music, annually reviewing over 1,000 works and releasing between 40 and 60 works for both choir and organ.

Video

Our DVDs offer spiritual help, healing, and biblical guidance for a broad range of life issues including grief and loss, marriage, forgiveness, facing death, understanding suicide, bullying, addictions, Alzheimer's, and Christian formation.

Learn more about us at our website:
www.paracletepress.com or phone us toll-free at 1.800.451.5006

SCAN TO READ MORE

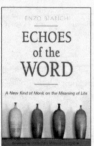